—PEOPLE TO KNOW—

HILLARY RODHAM CLINTON

Activist First Lady

T. J. Stacey

ENSLOW PUBLISHERS, INC.

44 Fadem Road	P.O. Box 38
Box 699	Aldershot
Springfield, N.J. 07081	Hants GU12 6BP
U.S.A.	U.K.

> *A special thank you to Judith Warner, author of* Hillary Clinton: The Inside Story, *and Dutton Signet, a division of Penguin USA, Inc., for their help with this book.*

Library of Congress Cataloging-in-Publication Data

Stacey, T. J.
   Hillary Rodham Clinton, Activist First Lady / T. J. Stacey.
      p. cm. — (People to know)
   Includes bibliographical references and index.
   ISBN 0-89490-583-X
   1. Clinton, Hillary Rodham—Juvenile literature. 2. Clinton, Bill, 1946- —Juvenile literature. 3. Presidents' spouses—United States—Biography—Juvenile literature. [1. Clinton, Hillary Rodham. 2. First ladies. 3. Women—Biography.] I. Title.
II. Series.
E887.C55S73 1994
973.929'092—dc20
[B]   94-5226
                                                          CIP
                                                           AC

Printed in the United States of America

10 9 8 7 6 5 4 3

Photo Credits: Scott Carpenter, *Arkansas Democratic Gazette*, pp. 6, 16, 34, 42, 65, 71, 75, 78, 80, 83, 85, 88, 95, 101; David Gottschalk, *Arkansas Democratic Gazette*, p. 113; Rick McFarland, *Arkansas Democratic Gazette*, p. 62; Ernest Ricketts, p. 18; The White House, p. 11.

Cover Photo: Courtesy of the White House.

Contents

In the new code of laws which I suppose it will be necessary for you to make I desire you would remember the ladies, and be more generous and favorable to them than your ancestors. Do not put such unlimited power into the hands of the husbands. Remember all men would be tyrants if they could. If particular care and attention is not paid to the ladies, we are determined to foment a rebellion, and will not hold ourselves bound by any laws in which we have no voice or representation.

—Abigail Adams,
in a letter to John Adams,
March 31, 1776

There is one secret, and it is the power we all have in forming our own destinies.

—Dolley Madison

The first lady reacts to a crowd of friends and supporters in Little
Rock in early 1993.

1

A Girl With High Sights

In the early 1960s, when she was a student at Ralph Waldo Emerson Junior High in Park Ridge, Illinois, Hillary Rodham decided she wanted to be an astronaut.

The Soviet Union had launched the first satellite, *Sputnik 1*, in October 1957. Then, in 1961, a Soviet cosmonaut became the first person to successfully orbit the earth. Americans were alarmed. The United States had not yet traveled into space at all. It was dangerous to allow the Soviets to get that far ahead. The United States had to catch up.

President John F. Kennedy focused on this challenge in his 1961 inauguration speech. He promised that the United States would take the lead in space. He also dared the nation to put a man on the moon by the end of the decade.

First the Soviets had to be overtaken. The future of the free world was at stake. It was important for students to study hard and gain knowledge. They would become scientists and engineers. They would develop the new technologies the United States space program needed to outdo the Soviets. Hillary and millions of other young Americans were filled with a sense of purpose. They were determined to learn all they could, and help America win the space race.

Hillary wanted to do more than study and invent things, though. She wanted to be one of the pioneers of outer space—a United States astronaut. It was a difficult goal. An astronaut had to have intelligence, inner strength, and the courage to go where others had never been. It would require a lot of hard work, but it would be worthwhile. By flying into space, Hillary would help her country beat the Soviets, and fulfill an important mission.

She wrote a letter to the National Aeronautics and Space Administration (NASA) and asked them how she should start preparing to be an astronaut. Someone wrote back, but it was not the reply Hillary expected. NASA's policy was that girls could not become astronauts.

This answer was "infuriating," Hillary told a reporter years later.[1] She resented being told that she couldn't achieve her dreams simply because she was a girl. That was not the message Hillary received from her parents.

"I felt very fortunate because, as a girl growing up, I never felt anything but support from my family," she told one interviewer. "Whatever I thought I could do or be, they supported. There was no distinction between me and my brothers, or any barriers thrown up to me that I couldn't think about doing something because I was a girl. It was just: If you work hard enough and you really apply yourself, then you should be able to do whatever you choose to do."[2]

Not everyone saw it that way. In the 1960s girls and women did not have all the options they have today. Hillary decided later that since her eyesight was not so great, she probably wouldn't have made a very good astronaut anyway.[3] In time she found other ways to make use of her talents and to serve her country.

She became a respected attorney and an advocate for children. She married Bill Clinton and helped him regain the Arkansas governorship. She gave birth to their daughter, Chelsea, in 1980. And in 1992, Bill Clinton was elected President of the United States, and Hillary Rodham Clinton became one of the most influential women in the world—America's first lady.

Historians will recognize Hillary as a transitional figure. First ladies have traditionally taken a passive role in the White House. Hillary did not. She arrived in Washington as an accomplished woman with her own political power, apart from her husband's. Working with him, she has used her power to get things done.

Early in his presidency, Bill Clinton gave Hillary the important and very difficult job of reorganizing the nation's troubled health care system. Putting the first lady to work in this way was unprecedented. Others before her, especially Eleanor Roosevelt, were known for their activism. But no other presidential wife has been as visibly active in official policy-making.

Who is this pioneering woman? How did Hillary Rodham Clinton become the person she is today? What motivates her and what are her goals?

Hillary is a very private person. Bit by bit, through interviews and her public actions, she is still revealing who she is. When we piece it together, the portrait emerges of a complex woman—a mother, spouse, career professional, and activist leader. She is a first lady who embodies the changing role of women in the 1990s.

Since her childhood, an important part of Hillary's life has been her religious faith. A favorite saying of hers, she told a reporter, is attributed to the founder of the Methodist church, John Wesley. It goes: "Do all the good you can, by all the means you can, in all the ways you can, at all the times you can, to all the people you can, as long as you ever can."[4]

Can someone be *that* good? Is Hillary for real? Or is she too good to be true? Many people, even those who don't know much about her, have strong opinions about her. She has a bold style. She is distinctly different from

Hillary Rodham Clinton.

her last few predecessors. Some people like her, others do not. But there is one point on which many of her critics and fans agree: Hillary Rodham Clinton has redefined the role of first lady.

This is the story of her life so far.

2

Park Ridge, U.S.A.

Park Ridge, Illinois, was like many American suburbs in the 1950s. It had quiet streets, big houses, and well-kept lawns. It was safe, the kind of place where people didn't bother to lock their doors. And there were children everywhere.

"There must have been 40 or 50 children within a four-block radius of our house, and within four years of Hillary's age," her mother, Dorothy Rodham, told a reporter for the *Washington Post*. "They were all together, all of the time, a big extended family."[1]

Hillary and her two younger brothers were among the youngsters who roamed the neighborhood as if it was one giant backyard. Growing up with dozens of friends, they played cops and robbers and hide-and-seek, checkers and Parcheesi.[2] All of these children were part of the Baby Boom, the population explosion that followed World War II.

It was a time of unprecedented prosperity, progress and optimism in America. Following the war, millions of soldiers went to college free on the G.I. bill. Then they entered the work force. By the 1950s, young and growing families like the Rodhams were sprouting in suburbs all around the country. The Rodham family was part of the middle class, and middle-class life was never more comfortable than in the 1950s.

American might had helped win the war. Now, in Park Ridge and other towns across the country, technology was improving the standard of American living. A new medium called television allowed families to bring the outside world right into their living rooms. Traveling out into that world became easier, as jet planes replaced the old propeller-driven airplanes taking off from O'Hare Airport, near Park Ridge. Scientists like Jonas Salk were developing new medicines that were wiping out horrible diseases like polio. Jobs were plentiful and the U.S. economy was robust. People could afford to enjoy leisure activities—golf, skiing, boating, and spectator sports—like never before.[3]

This was the world the Rodham family found in Park Ridge in 1950. That year they moved into a brick house at the corner of Wisner Road and Elm Street. It was also the year that Hillary's younger brother, Hugh, was born. Before that, Hillary had lived with her parents in a one-bedroom apartment in Chicago, her first home after she was born at Edgewater Hospital on October 26, 1947. Dorothy Rodham had chosen the name Hillary Diane. She thought Hillary sounded exotic and unusual. It was a man's name then, too. Derived from Latin, it means "cheerful."

The name fit Hillary well. Her mother remembers her daughter as being a good-natured baby. Even as an infant she had a tight focus. She liked solving problems. She also enjoyed books, and having her parents read to her.[4] She wasn't shy. As a toddler she didn't hesitate to fight with the neighbor kids if she felt they deserved it.

Another brother, Tony, was born in 1954, and the Rodham family was complete. Like their Park Ridge neighbors, they were neither rich nor poor, but somewhere in the middle. Hugh Rodham supported the family with his own drapery business. He designed, made, and installed drapes and curtains. He sold them to hotels and big companies.

Mr. Rodham worked hard. He had gone to Penn State on a football scholarship. He wanted to make sure his children had the opportunity to go to college, too.[5] By example, and through his encouragement, Mr. Rodham showed his children the value of hard work. He was a perfectionist, and some of it rubbed off on them. It wasn't his style to praise his children often. Instead he had a gruff demeanor. He pretended to be hard to please.

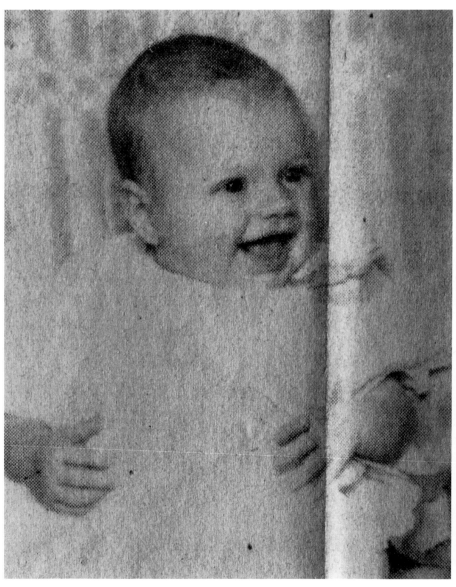

Hillary Rodham's baby photo, as it appeared years later in the *Arkansas Democrat*. She was born at Edgewater Hospital in Chicago in 1947, during the post-World War II baby boom.

"We were probably the only kids in the whole suburb who didn't get an allowance," Tony Rodham told *People*. "We'd rake the leaves, cut the grass, pull weeds, shovel snow. All your friends would be going to a movie. After your errands, you'd walk in and say, 'Gee, Dad, I could use two or three dollars.' He'd flop another potato on your dinner plate and say, 'That's your reward.' "[6]

The family still jokes about how Hillary would bring home a report card full of A's. Her mother would congratulate her. Then Hugh Rodham would look it over and say, "You must go to a pretty easy school."[7]

Actually, Hillary was a good student. First she attended Eugene Field Grammar School, then Ralph Waldo Emerson Junior High. Later she went to Maine East High School until her senior year when she went to the newly constructed Maine South High School. Throughout her school years in Park Ridge, Illinois, she was curious and hard-working. If she wasn't the top student in the class, she was always one of the best.[8] She credits her teachers who helped her get excited about learning.

"I had superb teachers," Hillary told *Parade*. "I had a sixth-grade teacher, Elisabeth King, who went on with me to junior high as an English teacher. She was so encouraging to us. She had us writing very long reports, because she insisted that we had to learn how to express ourselves. In junior high and high school, I had great

Hillary Rodham's sixth-grade class picture. Hillary is seated in the front row, far right side of the picture.

teachers of literature who exposed me to all kinds of people I had never thought of before."[9]

Perhaps the most important factor in her success at school was the encouragement she received from her mother. Dorothy Rodham gave Hillary the message that education was important.

"I explained to her very early that school was a great adventure," Mrs. Rodham told a French magazine, *Paris-Match*. "That she was going to learn great things, live new passions. I motivated her in a way that she wasn't resigned to go to school. I wanted her to be excited by the idea. Maybe that's why Hillary was never afraid. Not of school. Not of anything."[10]

She certainly had no fear of trying new things. She earned Girl Scout badges for many different activities. In the summertime she worked as a lifeguard at the neighborhood wading pool. She also took piano lessons. She learned to square dance and play Ping-Pong. In high school she took drama classes and debated.[11]

Hillary liked to organize things, too. She once staged a neighborhood version of the Olympic Games in the Rodhams' front yard. And she always enjoyed talking with friends. They debated things that many girls of her age were not interested in, like world events, politics, even sports.

"We used to sit on her front porch and solve the world's problems," said Ernest Ricketts, a neighbor and friend of Hillary's since they were eight years old. "She also knew all the players and stats, batting averages—Roger Maris, Mickey Mantle—everything about baseball."[12]

The Rodham family attended the First United Methodist Church, just a few blocks from their house. The people who went there followed the Methodist doctrine of showing their love for God by doing good works.

A new youth minister arrived at the church when Hillary was in ninth grade. His name was Don Jones, and he was from New York City. The Rev. Jones formed a youth group, and led the members in discussions. He took them on field trips, too. Sometimes he brought Hillary and other children out to the farms southwest of Park Ridge. There the suburban kids would help migrant families by baby-sitting while the parents worked the fields.

The church group also took bus trips to the inner city. They went to the south side of Chicago. There Hillary came into contact with people who led lives unlike her own. She met people from diverse ethnic backgrounds, including African Americans and Hispanics. She encountered others who didn't have all the advantages she had—students whose parents might not have been as supportive as hers. She met desperate kids who had joined gangs. Hillary talked with them, and began to realize she had much in common with them.

"Having my eyes opened as a teenager to other people and the way they live certainly affected me," she has said.[13]

Starting with those first experiences in her church's youth group, Hillary continued doing good works. As a high school sophomore, she organized a food drive for the hungry. She helped raise money for the poor, and ran a voter-registration project. She was learning that when she tried, she could make a difference. It was the beginning of a lifelong commitment to social activism.

The Rev. Jones also had a Thursday-night class, which his students called the University of Life.[14] They talked about civil rights and other social problems that were becoming more important in the early 1960s. Jones wanted his students to think about the larger world beyond Park Ridge. He invited them to consider how issues of justice and race affected them. He also tried to show them a link between religion and their everyday lives. Jones encouraged his students to read, even difficult books.

So at age 16, Hillary began reading works by great philosophers and theologians like Paul Tillich, Reinhold Niebuhr and Søren Kierkegaard.[15] Jones also introduced her to the work of the poet e. e. cummings, the paintings of Pablo Picasso, and the writings of Albert Camus and others.

Hillary tried to learn what she could from these great minds, and enjoyed discussing their works. Even then, she was not afraid to assert herself, said Jones, who is now a religion professor at Drew University.

"Hillary wasn't going to take a back seat to anyone," he said. "She wouldn't let some young man dominate the meetings if he had nothing to say. She wasn't going to be demure and spend a lot of time looking cute to attract people."[16]

One Sunday in 1962, Jones took the group into downtown Chicago to hear a man speak. Afterwards, Jones brought the students backstage and introduced them one by one to the speaker. He was Martin Luther King, Jr. Even today, Hillary remembers that day vividly.[17]

Hillary's interest in politics was obvious by her junior year, when she was elected vice president of her class. The next year she ran for president of the senior class, but lost. Her interest in government extended beyond school, however. She was also fascinated with national politics. That fall she organized a mock political convention at school. It was complete with nominating speeches, posters, and demonstrations.

As a teenager, Hillary followed her father's political convictions. She supported the conservative Republican candidate Barry Goldwater in the 1964 presidential election. She worked for the Goldwater campaign that fall. She even wore a sash that said "Goldwater Girl."[18]

In her senior year Hillary was named a National Merit Scholar for finishing in the top 5 percent of her class academically. She was voted the girl most likely to succeed.[19] That wasn't a surprise. Anyone could see that she was smart. She also had an inquisitive personality that people liked. She was sincerely interested in all sorts of things. There was something else about Hillary too. She didn't pay too much attention to her appearance.

"She had absolutely no vanity," said high school classmate Jeanie Snodgrass Almo. "She was totally unconcerned with how she appeared to people—and she was loved for that."[20]

Not that she was careless or sloppy. Like other girls, she wore pleated skirts, crisp blouses, loafers, and knee socks.[21] With her blonde hair and blue eyes, Hillary didn't need makeup to be attractive. She was naturally pretty, and she was certain of who she was. Worrying about her looks would have been a waste of time.

Hillary had a large circle of male and female friends. They went to football and basketball games and dances together. Like her, they were young people looking to the future. They were not likely to get themselves in much trouble. Often a dozen or more would gather at the house of Hillary's good friend Betsy Johnson to watch TV and talk.[22]

Sometimes Hillary sensed a difference between her thinking and that of her friends. Years later, she told a reporter: "I saw a lot of my friends who had been really lively and smart and doing well in school beginning to worry that boys would think they were too smart, or beginning to cut back on how well they did or the courses they took, because that's not where their boyfriends were. And I can recall thinking, 'Gosh, why are they doing that?' It didn't make sense to me."[23]

So she didn't focus too much on appearances. Nor did she set any limits for herself. There were too many things she was interested in, too many things she wanted to do. A girl who planned to stay in Park Ridge might worry about appearing too smart. Hillary Rodham had other plans.

3

The 1960s:
Years of Change

In 1965, Hillary's immediate plan was to attend college. It was her senior year at Maine South High. Many of her friends were applying to colleges and universities in the Chicago area. They wanted to be close to Park Ridge and their families and friends. Hillary could have chosen a nearby college, too, but she had learned through all her activities in high school to keep herself open to opportunities. One presented itself that year.

"My senior year I had two young teachers—one had graduated from Wellesley and the other graduated from Smith," she told interviewer Charles Allen. Both women were graduate students in education at Northwestern University.

"They'd been assigned to teach in my high school, and they were so bright and smart and terrific teachers, and they lobbied me hard to apply to those schools, which I had never thought of before," said Hillary. "And then when I was accepted, they lobbied me hard to go and be able to work out all of the financial and other issues. So I went to Wellesley."[1]

That fall her father loaded up the family car and drove Hillary from Park Ridge to the Wellesley campus, just outside Boston. Her mother came along.

"Aside from a few trips away with girlfriends, Hillary hadn't really been away from home," Dorothy Rodham told a reporter. "I loved having my kids around, and when she went to Wellesley, well, it was really, really hard to leave her."[2]

For Hillary it was the start of a new adventure. Suddenly, she was far from the familiar, comfortable world of Park Ridge. Wellesley, a beautiful campus with trees and scenic walks, was one of the best women's colleges in the country. Hillary arrived in time for an interesting college experience.

By 1965, the calm prosperity of the 1950s was long gone. President Kennedy's assassination in 1963 had shattered the nation's sense of well-being. Before his death, Kennedy addressed one of the most pressing issues of the time. He had proposed far-reaching civil rights legislation. If passed by Congress it would guarantee equal rights for African Americans. But halfway through the decade the country was still deeply divided over race.

In Alabama, Martin Luther King, Jr. was leading marches for school desegregation. It was just two years since Hillary had met him in Chicago, and by the time she graduated from Wellesley in 1969, King would be dead—killed by an assassin's bullet. Malcolm X and Robert F. Kennedy would be gunned down, too. The assassinations ignited large-scale riots in several cities.

Meanwhile, students at many colleges and universities were beginning to protest the war in Vietnam. The conflict had begun quietly and continued for nearly ten years. Yet the purpose of sending U.S. troops to Southeast Asia was never clearly understood. To many people it seemed a senseless war. But as it dragged on, more troops were sent and more young men were killed.

Frustrated, many in the younger generation took to the streets in protest. They marched against the war and racial injustice. They fought "the system" that allowed these things to happen. It was a era of turmoil. At times it seemed as if American society might collapse. This charged atmosphere affected everyone. The young women of Wellesley did their best to keep up.

"We had the assassinations of the leaders, we had the loss of hope and expectations about progress, we had the war and all the teach-ins," Alan Schechter, one of Hillary's professors, told writer Judith Warner. "It really was a moment in American history that was unique in terms of problems confronting society."³

Many people Hillary's age reacted by rejecting their parents' values. Often they talked about changing the world. They had their own new music to help them define their identity. It was called rock and roll. Many older people didn't appreciate the searing guitars and driving beat of rock music. But they could hardly avoid it. The baby boomers had powerful new stereos. They didn't just listen to their music. They played their records at a volume you could *feel* in your chest. The lyrics often made a statement too. When the Rolling Stones sang, "I can't get no satisfaction. . ." they spoke for the generation coming of age in the 1960s.

The boomers were questioning old ways of thinking. When they were children in the 1950s, it had seemed that things were always improving. But as they became young adults, many started to feel that something was missing. Now they challenged the very idea of progress.

"The late '60s were an exciting, wonderful time to be in school, because we spent days upon end worrying, talking, and carrying on about what was happening," Hillary told *Parade*.⁴

College campuses everywhere were becoming centers of change. Some young people rebelled outright. They experimented with drugs and sex. They ignored rules set down by the law and their parents. It was an exciting time to be a college student, but it was a troublesome time too. The turbulence was distressing for parents with children away at school. Back in Park Ridge, Dorothy Rodham was concerned.

"I was worried about her, but Hillary adjusted to Wellesley without a problem," said Dorothy Rodham. "She joined clubs and was immediately active."[5] She became president of the Young Republicans.[6] That didn't last long, however. Hillary's support of conservative Barry Goldwater had been inherited from her father. Like most people, she started out seeing the world through the eyes of her parents. In Hillary's case, that meant accepting traditional Republican positions: Keep government spending and taxes as low as possible; let people solve problems by working through local government.

Those ideas had made sense to Hillary in Park Ridge. At Wellesley she had the opportunity to decide for herself what she thought. She read more books. She continued to debate important issues in classes and with her friends.

Many young people were becoming more aware of problems in American society. All they had to do was watch the evening news. Angry people were marching in the streets. Young Americans were dying of war wounds on the other side of the world. The nation's leaders were being shot down.

Martin Luther King's assassination had an especially

powerful impact on Hillary. Johanna Branson was her roommate then. She remembers the day it happened.

"People don't usually see Hillary get upset. I saw her very upset that afternoon. I was alone in our suite. She came in, the door flew back, and her book bag went crashing against the wall. She was completely distraught about the horror of it. I know it sounds corny, but I believe that's when she resolved to be more involved in changing injustice."[7]

The event may have hardened Hillary's resolve. But she had always been a problem-solver. Over her college career she looked for ways to address issues of injustice. Perhaps government could actively help solve some social problems. Hillary seemed to think so, and she wanted to be involved.

By 1968 she had rejected her Republican roots. That year she campaigned for Democratic presidential candidate Hubert Humphrey. It was a reversal of her previous political position, but it was in keeping with her character.

"There was a great deal of change going on in the country, and she reflected some of it," said Jeff Shields. Now an attorney in Chicago, he dated Hillary during her first year at Wellesley. "From the first time I met her, I remember being struck by her real interest in government, from the point of view of someone who wanted to be involved and have an impact, but didn't know exactly how," he told author Judith Warner.[8]

Hillary had not radically changed her outlook. She still knew she had to work hard to succeed. She still believed that strong family ties were important. But she had also been exposed to diversity. She had met people unlike herself, and found that she shared much in common with them. She was not afraid of them, and she wanted to help.

As she told reporter Dotson Rader in 1993: "I was raised to be self-reliant and to be responsible, but to know that I was part of a larger community to which I also have responsibilities. . . . I've always believed, and this goes back to their [her parents] teaching and my church, that because I was blessed enough to be healthy and have a strong, supportive family, I had an obligation to care for other people, to help them. It wasn't something you did as an afterthought. It was how you lived."[9]

Living that way, she saw how the system was not working equally well for everyone. Some people weren't getting the basic opportunities they needed to succeed. Hillary knew what it was like to want something badly—to be an astronaut, for instance—and to be denied the opportunity.

Her excellent education would give Hillary a good shot at overcoming some of the unfairness she faced as a woman. She would pursue her own personal successes, but Hillary had other goals in mind too. Since her work with the Rev. Jones in junior high school, she had demonstrated her desire to make a difference in people's lives.

At Wellesley, she continued her volunteer work. She traveled to Boston to help poor children learn to read. She also became active in student government. Her skills as a leader continued to develop. As in high school, she studied hard and earned good grades. She focused on what interested her most, and majored in political science.

Hillary liked to have fun as well. She went to Harvard football games with her boyfriend Jeff Shields. They went to parties, and to dances at his Harvard dorm. Hillary especially liked to dance to the music of the Supremes. At parties she was easygoing—the kind of person who was comfortable talking with anyone else in the room.

"She was not overly bookish, or interested in grades, or committed to studying too hard," said Schechter, her political science professor. "She was a warm, friendly, outgoing, smiling, relaxed person."[10]

As a junior, Hillary worked as a counselor, helping freshmen adapt to college life. Again, she met people from backgrounds different from her own. She was becoming a popular and trusted person on the Wellesley campus. She helped other students, and soon they helped her in return.

In her senior year Hillary was elected president of the student body. Her ability to relate to all kinds of people was a valuable skill. Whenever there was a conflict, she seemed to be there, helping solve the problem. And there were plenty of conflicts on college campuses in the 1960s. Hillary organized the first teach-ins on the Vietnam War at Wellesley. These were long informal meetings. Professors and students talked about what was happening in Southeast Asia.

In the spring of 1969 she was chosen by her classmates to speak at their commencement. This was a first for Wellesley. The idea came up in Hillary's constitutional law class.[11] There had been many changes at the school over the previous four years. It seemed fitting to break tradition somehow. A good way to do that would be to have a student speak at graduation on behalf of the senior class. That's what Hillary's classmates thought.

At first, the president of the college did not agree. But after the idea was approved by the entire student body, the president reconsidered. The students just had to find a speaker who was acceptable to the school's administration. Hillary was the one.

So, four years after he had first delivered his daughter there, Hugh Rodham drove back to Wellesley. This time Hillary's mother stayed at home. Mr. Rodham looked forward to seeing his daughter speak to her classmates. But he probably wasn't expecting the speech she gave.

Hillary took the podium immediately after Senator Edward Brooke of Massachusetts. The senator had

Hillary Rodham as she appeared in her college yearbook. She went to Wellesley College, outside Boston, after one of her high school teachers urged her to apply there.

delivered a typical graduation speech. It might have been enough in 1959, but it didn't satisfy Wellesley's class of 1969. They felt they had been through something that had never happened before. They wanted a message that would help them put it in perspective. The senator's talk didn't do it. To Hillary, his speech seemed irrelevant, and she told him so.

The parents and faculty in the audience did not expect to hear a fresh graduate of Wellesley publicly criticize a U.S. senator. There were a few gasps.[12] But Hillary couldn't be stopped. She ignored her prepared speech for a few minutes in order to scold the senator. It was if the younger generation was telling its parents, "See, this is what we mean . . ." Then she started her address: "The challenge now is to practice politics as the art of making what appears to be impossible, possible. . . ."

That opening statement defined Hillary's personality and her approach. She was idealistic, yet practical. The speech that followed was sometimes rambling. But it captured the mood of the late 1960s. And it was relevant to her classmates.

"We are, all of us, exploring a world that none of us understands, and [we are] attempting to create within that uncertainty," she told the crowd. "But there are some things we feel, feelings that our prevailing, acquisitive, and competitive corporate life, including tragically, the universities, is not the way of life for us.

We're searching for more immediate, ecstatic, and penetrating modes of living."[13]

The women of Wellesley gave her a standing ovation. The speech was covered in *Life* magazine. The story carried excerpts from graduation speeches around the nation, next to a picture of Hillary.[14] In fact, her remarks were tame compared with those of some other speakers. Some speeches were extremely pessimistic. Others were cynical.

Her address to the Wellesley graduates was more realistic. But it was also a passionate call to action. In fact, the last line of her speech pointed the way to the next step on Hillary Rodham's path:

"You and I must be free not to save the world in a glorious crusade," she said, "but to practice with all the skill of our being, the art of making possible."

4

The Law of Attraction

Hillary Rodham had earned her degree, with high honors, from a well-regarded college. Her adult life lay ahead. What would she do next? She had stated her case in the Wellesley commencement speech. But how do you begin to make the impossible possible?

It was clear to Hillary that the world could be a better place. She was also certain that it was her duty to try to make it so. She had the right tools to get things accomplished. She was energetic and bright, with a strong personality. Her leadership abilities were impressive, and she was not afraid to challenge authority.

Now she just had to get started. There would be obstacles, however. In the 1960s many people still had a difficult time accepting the reality of a young woman with political power. Hillary had worked hard to prove herself at Wellesley. Yet often she wasn't taken seriously. In fact, her mother has said that Hillary's college career was the most difficult stage of her daughter's life—worse even than the 1992 presidential campaign.

"People gave her a hard time because she wanted to be the best," Mrs. Rodham told *Paris-Match*. "I think that those years were those of her greatest challenge. She was a young woman and was the equal of men. At that time that wasn't yet accepted."[1]

Indeed, many more doors were closed to American women in the 1960s than today. But Hillary was determined to do what she wanted, whether it was accepted or not. She was intelligent and capable. She felt strongly that she had the right to pursue any job or life she desired.

So she took the next logical step for a recent college graduate with an interest in politics. It was a choice that would allow her to make use of her talents, and fulfill a deeply felt duty.

"All during my growing-up years I had a combined message of personal opportunity but also public responsibility—that there were obligations that people who were as lucky as I was owed society," she has said.[2]

Hillary had heard John F. Kennedy deliver a stirring message in his inauguration speech. "Ask not what your country can do for you, ask what you can do for your country," said Kennedy. For Hillary, the answer was to become a lawyer. She would go to law school, and discover how to work within the system. Then she could address some of the injustices she saw in her country.

Specifically, Hillary was interested in helping the underprivileged. At Wellesley she had written her senior thesis on community action programs for the poor. Her paper compared short- and long-term programs to determine which had a more lasting effect on the lives of the participants. The paper earned A's from all four of the professors who graded it.[3] It also sharpened Hillary's focus before she continued her education.

When the time came to send out law school applications, Hillary aimed high. She wanted to go to the best school possible. She considered Harvard, but she decided on the law school at Yale. Years later she told a reporter for an Arkansas newspaper about an experience that helped make up her mind.

"I met a very distinguished, older law professor, and my friend who attended Harvard Law School said 'Professor So-and-so, this is my friend. She's trying to decide whether to come here next year or attend our closest competitor.' "

"This tall, rather imposing professor . . . looked down at me and said, 'Well, first of all, we don't have any close competitors. Second, we don't need any more women.' That's what made my decision. I was leaning toward Yale anyway, but that fellow's comments iced the cake."[4]

Alan Schechter, her professor at Wellesley, wrote a

letter of recommendation for Hillary to the admissions office at the Yale Law School. In it he praised her highly. He also made a prediction.

"Hillary Rodham is by far the most outstanding young woman I have taught in the seven years I have been on the Wellesley College faculty," he wrote. "I have high hopes for Hillary and for her future. She has the intellectual ability, personality, and character to make a remarkable contribution to American society."[5]

Before she started at Yale—and set out to make Schechter's words come true—Hillary took a summer off and went to Alaska. There she worked at several odd jobs. She even had a stint in a fish processing plant. One day she told the owner that some of the fish looked bad. It looked as if it might not be fit to eat, she told him. That was the end of Hillary's career in fish processing.[6]

That fall she entered Yale. There she would meet and merge paths with two people, each of whom would become vitally important in her life.

As a first-year law student in the spring of 1970, Hillary read in *Time* magazine about Marian Wright Edelman, founder of the Children's Defense Fund. Then she saw a flyer on a campus bulletin board, announcing that Edelman was coming to speak at Yale. Hillary went to listen. Edelman talked about her mission: to act as an advocate for the nation's underprivileged youth. During the speech Hillary was struck with an idea.

"I knew right away that I had to go to work for her," she told a group of students years later.[7] After the talk, Hillary introduced herself to Edelman and asked if she could work for her that summer. Edelman was not very encouraging. She did not have a big budget, she told Hillary. There was not enough money to pay a summer intern.

Hillary was determined, though. She did some research, then wrote a grant proposal. The grant came through, and she funded her own position as a summer intern for Edelman's organization. Hillary was assigned to work with a Senate subcommittee that was studying conditions in migrant labor camps.[8] She interviewed workers and their families. She saw how children were affected by the conditions in the camps. It was exactly the kind of work she wanted.

Hillary was an active law student, which was no surprise. Somehow she got her own key to the Yale Law School Library so she could study late at night. She served on the editorial board of the *Yale Review of Law and Social Action*, a journal that is no longer published. She also became an unofficial student leader.

Her classmates remember how she led a large meeting as a first-year law student. The school was in turmoil over the trial of some of the Black Panthers. The Black Panther Party for Self-Defense was founded by Bobby Seale and others in Oakland, California, in 1966. The Black Panthers did not practice Martin Luther

Hillary has changed her hair and her look many times over the years.
Here she appears at the dedication of a new auditorium in 1984.

King's approach of non-violence, instead choosing aggressive confrontations and pressure tactics to achieve their goals. Members of the group were being tried in a courthouse just off the Yale campus. There were demonstrations every day. It was becoming impossible for students to concentrate on their work. Many students sympathized with the Black Panthers, and talked about going on strike. But the faculty wanted the law school to keep functioning normally.[9]

Angry students gathered in an auditorium to discuss what they should do. Hillary sat up front on the stage with several older male students. She was the youngest, and the only woman, but she ended up moderating the meeting.[10] She made sure that each speaker got the chance to say what he or she wanted. She helped them clarify their feelings, and gradually steered the entire group toward a constructive solution. Years later, her former classmates still remember the leadership Hillary showed in that meeting.

"She had complete self-possession," said Carolyn Ellis, a friend of Hillary's. "Everybody walked out of the room. We can no longer remember what the meeting was about—we can only remember we were awed by her."[11]

Law school seemed to be the right place for Hillary, and the early 1970s was an exciting time to be a law student. It was still an era of wrenching social change.

On top of the Vietnam War and racial issues, the women's movement had picked up steam. Women across the nation were demanding equal rights. There were new opportunities for a young woman with a law degree from Yale.

At the same time, many young people were talking about dropping out of society. Some actually did. Others, like Hillary, decided to stay and work for change within the system. Sometimes they were criticized for this. Hillary remembered what it was like during a speech to her former classmates at a Yale Law School alumni gathering in October 1992.

"There was a great amount of ferment and confusion about what was and wasn't the proper role of law school education," she said. "We would have great arguments about whether we were selling out because we were getting a law degree, whether in fact we should be doing something else, not often defined clearly, but certainly passionately argued. That we should somehow be 'out there,' wherever 'there' was, trying to help solve the problems that took up so much of our time in argument and discussion. . . .Those were difficult and turbulent times."[12]

Despite these distractions, Hillary kept her focus on a law degree. This goal held a special challenge. In the early 1970s there was still an invisible barrier that Hillary and other young women were attempting to overcome. The law was a profession that traditionally was closed to women. If a woman worked in the law, it was almost always as a secretary or clerk.

Hillary was out to change that. Since childhood, she had believed it was her right to pursue whatever she could imagine for herself—in professional life and in her personal life. She believed she deserved the same opportunities that others enjoyed. Following that path had led her to the Yale Law School, and she expected equal opportunities once she got out of school.

In the meantime, she was not afraid to create her own opportunities. Hillary sometimes bent the rules that others were compelled to follow. Sometimes she created her own good luck.

An example is the story of how Hillary met Bill Clinton. She did not wait for something to happen, she seized the moment and made it happen. It's the stuff of which movie scripts are made.

As the story goes, they saw each other in a class one day at Yale. Bill Clinton followed Hillary out, but wasn't brave enough to introduce himself. She had noticed him, too. He was the one she overheard bragging to another student that Arkansas was home to the biggest watermelons in the world. They spotted each other again in the Yale Law School Library. Both of them have repeated the story many times. They still argue over the exact details—like where he was standing.[13] Bill Clinton told his version to Charles Allen:

> This guy was trying to talk me into joining the *Yale Law Review* and telling me that I could clerk for the U.S. Supreme Court . . . and then I could go on to New York and make a ton of money. And I kept telling him that I didn't want to do all of that. I wanted to go home to Arkansas. . . . And all the time I was talking to this guy I was looking at Hillary at the other end of the library. And the Yale Law School Library is a real long, narrow [room]. She was down at the other end, and . . . I just was staring at her. . . . And she closed this book, and she walked all the way down the library . . . and she came up to me and she said, 'Look, if you're going to keep staring at me, and I'm going to keep staring back, I think we should at least know each other. I'm Hillary Rodham. What's your name?'

Clinton was at a loss for words. For a moment he couldn't even tell her his name.

"I was so embarrassed," he said. "But I was real impressed that she did that. And we've been together, more or less, ever since."[14]

Hillary was not shy. As her mother had observed years before, she wasn't afraid of anything. Asked what drew her to Bill Clinton, she told *Parade*:

> He's a very attractive man. In those days he was very attractive, and I knew nothing about him. But

46

what I learned quickly was that he was unlike anyone I ever met—and still is. Because he combined an absolutely extraordinary mind with a huge heart. It is just not that usual to find people with both those great gifts that he had in such abundance. And we just started talking and never stopped. I guess that's the best way to say it. We are still talking.[15]

They didn't know, when they began talking in the library that day, how their conversation would change their lives and the course of the entire country.

5

The Man from Hope

As a law student at Yale, Bill Clinton was famous for talking about Arkansas.[1] He was proud of his home state and eager to impress people with interesting facts, like the watermelon story, for instance.

Hillary probably did not care much about watermelons. But she was deeply interested in politics, and so was Bill Clinton. One of their first dates included a long talk about foreign policy in Africa.[2]

The two young law students impressed each other. They shared an enthusiasm for public service, and they were both bright, idealistic, and articulate. Talking together, they exercised and expanded their powers of intellect. It was obvious that they made an excellent team.

Dorothy Rodham remembers when her daughter

first brought Bill Clinton back to Park Ridge. She couldn't believe the lively dinnertime discussions: "It was always the same subjects: Arkansas! American society! They never stopped thinking. They were amazing. We could listen to them for hours on end because they spoke from their hearts, and they were really concerned with people. They had a very humanist vision of America."[3]

Hillary and Bill did share a regard for the dignity and well-being of others. They cared about people. They also both saw government as an opportunity to work for positive change. Moreover, they weren't just big talkers, they were doers. Each had been active in student government. They were also keenly interested in national affairs.

For now they discussed society's problems. But both were eager to make their marks in the world beyond Yale. They were full of energy and plans for the future. In each other they found a sounding board—an ideal person on whom to test ideas. As their dialogue continued, Hillary and Bill began to build trust between themselves.

They talked about their ambitions and dreams. They had come to Yale from different backgrounds. Growing up in suburban Chicago, Hillary enjoyed the full support of both parents. Clinton was born in Hope, a small town in rural Arkansas. He always received strong encouragement from his mother, but his stepfather was an alcoholic who was at times abusive.[4]

They had distinctly different personalities, too. Hillary was methodical, rational, driven. Bill Clinton also was an achiever, but his style was more laid-back and intuitive, and he had plenty of southern charm. At Yale he had long hair and a beard. A saxophone player, he was known for his Elvis Presley impersonations. He was a "people" person. He loved to listen to and talk with others for hours.

Clinton began to set his course in earnest at age 17. That year he ran for Boys Nation, a group that teaches students about the electoral process. He was elected as a delegate, and traveled to the White House. There he met his idol, President John F. Kennedy. The Arkansas teenager returned home knowing he wanted to be involved in politics.[5]

Later, Clinton attended Georgetown University. After graduating he traveled to England as a Rhodes Scholar. Named for Cecil J. Rhodes, who made a fortune in diamond mining in South Africa, these scholarships allow outstanding students from the United States and former British colonies to study for two or three years at Oxford University, one of the finest universities in the world. Clinton took advantage of this opportunity to develop his mind. His best friend at Oxford was Strobe Talbott, who later became a reporter for *Time*. Talbott described Clinton as talented and compassionate.

"He was quite outstanding, even as a very young

man, for the way in which he combined a very obvious and eloquent idealism—that is, a passionate interest in the large issues that are involved in public policy—with a practical sense of politics. . . . He was very interested in both the cosmic and the nitty-gritty."[6]

A friend from high school who visited Clinton at Oxford was impressed with the way he soaked up facts.

"He is almost a fanatic about information," said Paul David Leopoulos. "He gathers it and retains it better than anyone I've ever known. He is fascinated with everything and knowledgeable about so many things."[7]

Clinton loved the stimulating learning environment at Oxford. But he turned down a third year there in order to accept a scholarship to the Yale Law School. There he would have the fateful encounter with Hillary Rodham in the library.

As Hillary saw immediately, Bill Clinton had a rare blend of brain power and compassion. He also knew himself well. In the early 1970s, many men still felt threatened by a strong woman like Hillary. Perhaps they feared that their own accomplishments might be overshadowed by the success of a brilliant woman. Clinton didn't feel that way. He accepted Hillary as a friend and an ally. He was not afraid of her, and she appreciated that.[8]

Hillary was sure of herself, too. Since childhood she had fought sexism. She may have sensed that she was not very welcome in the "man's world" of 1970s law and politics. To put her faith in a man—any man—might have felt risky. But Hillary Rodham was not afraid to take the right risks. So she and Bill Clinton kept talking.

She was focused. He cared about people. Both of them were smart, and interested in dedicating themselves to public policy. It didn't take them long to establish a bond that would grow stronger over the years. Soon their Yale Law School classmates noticed that Bill and Hillary had become a couple.

During Hillary's third year at Yale, they moved into a small house in New Haven together. It became a gathering spot where other law students came to have dinner, listen to music, and talk until all hours.[9] They discussed politics, of course. They also talked about what they would do in the future.

When that topic came up, there was some uncertainty between Bill and Hillary, despite the powerful attraction they had for each other. Both were committed to serving the public. But Bill Clinton had a unique vision of how he would perform his service. He had promised himself that after his education he would go back to Arkansas and help the people there.[10]

Would Hillary go there with him? Considering everything she had going for her, Arkansas did not offer much. After earning a law degree from Yale, she could find work at virtually any law firm she chose. Or she could work for the Children's Defense Fund in Washington. But what would a well-connected, high-powered Yale Law School graduate do in a southern, mostly rural state like Arkansas? Bill Clinton thought about it, and it concerned him.

"I loved being with her, but I had very ambivalent feelings about getting involved with her," he told *Vanity Fair* magazine. He says he told her on their earliest dates, "You know, I'm really worried about falling in love with you, because you're a great person, you could have a great life. If you wanted to run for public office, you could be elected, but I've got to go home. It's just who I am."[11]

Hillary was still finding the right path for herself. She was not going to rush into anything. But her path and Bill Clinton's seemed to be merging into one. In the summer of 1972, they both traveled to Texas, where Clinton managed George McGovern's unsuccessful presidential campaign. Hillary worked in San Antonio, registering Hispanic voters.[12]

When they returned to Yale that fall, Hillary decided to stay there for another year. She was a year ahead of Clinton, so she could have graduated and started a job search. Instead she stayed on, and studied at the Yale Child Study Center through a law school program. She worked with several experts, including child psychoanalyst Anna Freud, daughter of Sigmund Freud. Part of her job was to observe children at play. Watching them, she learned about normal childhood development. She helped research two books on children's rights, and strengthened her qualifications as an expert in that field.[13]

Hillary graduated from law school in 1973. She worked for the Children's Defense Fund for a few months. Then, early in 1974, both Hillary and Bill received a great opportunity.

The Watergate scandal was unfolding in Washington, D.C. There were accusations that the Nixon administration had been involved in illegal wiretapping and breaking into the Democratic National Committee headquarters in the Watergate apartment complex. The House Judiciary Subcommittee was looking into the allegations. The man leading the subcommittee's investigation needed five sharp young lawyers. He called Burke Marshall, a well-known law professor at Yale and the former assistant attorney general for civil rights in the Kennedy administration. Marshall recommended Hillary Rodham, Bill Clinton, and a few others.

Clinton declined. It was time for him to go home to Arkansas. But the offer was too good for Hillary to turn down. She accepted it and went to Washington. She was the perfect person for the job, said Marshall.

"It required a very good lawyer, young but very good," he said. "It also required someone who would keep her work to herself, or within the work of that group, so it required someone with judgment and sense.

Hillary had a broad scope of mind and very sound judgment."[14]

It was a grueling assignment. Hillary was part of a team of 43 lawyers. They worked 18-hour days, seven days a week, for months. Their job was to assemble evidence and put it in a form that the House Judiciary Subcommittee could use. They were not making judgments, they were just organizing information. House members would then decide if impeachment hearings against President Richard M. Nixon should proceed.

It was an exciting time for Hillary. She was taking part in a dramatic episode in U.S. history. Years later, she remembered how strange it all seemed.

"I was kind of locked in this soundproof room with the big headphones on, listening to tapes," she told the *Arkansas Gazette*. "There was one we called the tape of tapes. It was Nixon taping himself listening to the tapes, making up his defenses to what he heard on the tapes. So you would hear Nixon talk and then you'd hear very faintly the sound of a taped prior conversation with [Nixon aides] Haldeman and Ehrlichman. . . . And then you'd hear him say, 'What I meant when I said that was . . .' I mean, it was surreal, unbelievable."[15]

An important part of Hillary's job was to remain objective. She might have disagreed with the Nixon administration's position on many things, but she did not let her politics influence her work for the House

Judiciary Subcommittee. The legal team's job ended prematurely when Nixon resigned the presidency on August 8, 1974, partly as a result of their work.

In a speech to her Yale Law School classmates years later, Hillary recalled the job as a highlight of her professional life:

> Never have I been prouder to be a lawyer and to be an American than I was during those months . . . as we struggled to define the constitutional meaning of impeachment and to carry out our obligations with the highest professional standards. It was a great relief, and I thought, a great credit to the president, when President Nixon resigned. But it was also a resounding victory for the system that I had studied and learned about.[16]

In 1974, Hillary Rodham was 26. She had just played a role in the nation's most sensational legal case involving a public official. Her own career had not even begun, yet, with her credentials, she could write her own ticket. If she wanted, she could take a position with a big law firm and make lots of money. Some of her friends thought she ought to consider running for office. Or she could pursue her interest in children's rights. The years of schooling had prepared her well. Hillary now had many options.

Meanwhile, Bill Clinton was waiting in Arkansas.

6

The Politics of Romance

Hillary Rodham and Bill Clinton stayed in touch after he returned to his home state. He was teaching at the University of Arkansas Law School while she worked on the impeachment inquiry in Washington. They missed each other.[1] But, as Hillary said, they never stopped talking, even when they were several states apart. Between them they racked up some large phone bills in the first half of 1974.[2]

Then, in August, Hillary's assignment in Washington came to an end. She had to decide what to do next. Her career was ready to take off. But now there was a huge question confronting Hillary in her personal life: What would she and Bill Clinton do? Would they continue to have a long-distance relationship? There wasn't much doubt that they would stay involved with each other somehow. Everyone who knew them could see that a powerful bond had developed.

"He loved Hillary so much at Yale," said Clinton's mother, Virginia Kelley. "He was really concerned about whether she really would be happy in Arkansas, or would even come. But he told her going in, he said, 'I promised myself a long time ago, if the people of Arkansas will let me, I'll break my back to help my state.' And he said, 'That's my life. And that's the way it has to be for me.' "[3]

Hillary had her dreams, too. With her Yale law degree and her experience in Washington, she was in a good position to be an effective advocate for children. And there were other things to consider. Her parents still lived back in Park Ridge. She also had a whole network of friends she had met at Wellesley and Yale. Many of them were launching careers on the East Coast. But she wanted to keep Bill Clinton in her life, and he was teaching law in Fayetteville, Arkansas.

"I was very unsure of where I wanted to be," she has said. "I certainly was not ready to move completely to Arkansas yet, because I just didn't know whether that would be a decision that Bill would stick to. I really didn't know what to expect."[4]

Hillary had visited Arkansas in 1973. On that trip, Bill Clinton did his best to impress her with his home state's charms.

"He picked me up at the airport in Little Rock," she told *Newsweek* magazine. "He lived in Hot Springs, which was, like, an hour away. We drove eight hours. He took me to all these places he thought were beautiful. We went to all the state parks. We went to all the overlooks. And then we'd stop at his favorite barbecue place. Then we'd go down the road and stop at his favorite fried-pie place. My head was reeling. . . ."[5]

So she had seen the state already. She knew the pace of life there was more relaxed than in the nation's capital. She was also ready for a change after the stress of working on the impeachment inquiry. What's more, she had found a career opportunity in Arkansas.

"I really didn't know what I wanted to do, but I wanted to get out of Washington. I was exhausted, I had been working 18-, 20-hour days. And when I had visited Bill, I had met the dean of the law school at Fayetteville and he had said to me, 'If you ever want to teach, let me know.' So I figured what the heck, it wouldn't hurt. So I picked up the phone."[6]

The law school had an opening for a job teaching criminal law. It was hers if she wanted it. It wasn't Hillary's dream job, but it promised to be interesting. She would also be charged with running a legal aid clinic. And she would set up a program that gave students experience working with prison inmates. She decided to give Arkansas a try.

Hillary's friend Sara Ehrman gave her a ride from Washington to Fayetteville. They had met in Texas, working for the McGovern campaign. Hillary had lived in Ehrman's house while she was in Washington. They packed Hillary's belongings into Ehrman's car. Then Ehrman spent the long drive south and west trying to talk her friend out of making the move.

"I told her every 20 minutes that she was crazy to bury herself in Fayetteville," Ehrman told the *Washington Post.* She remembers telling Hillary: "You are crazy. You are out of your mind. You're going to this rural, remote place—and wind up married to some country lawyer."[7]

Ehrman was not the only one who thought Hillary was off her rocker. Most of her friends considered Arkansas the end of the earth. But Hillary had her own reasons for going. She told *Newsweek:*

"In '74, he'd asked me to marry him, and he said, 'I know this is a really hard choice because I'm committed to living in Arkansas.' And I'd say, 'Yeah it's a really hard choice.' And I finally just decided, you know, this is no way to make a decision. When you love somebody, you just have to go and see what it's like. So I moved to Arkansas and started teaching at the law school."[8]

Clinton, then 28, was making his first run for public office when Hillary arrived in August of 1974. He was a Democrat trying to unseat a popular Republican congressman against the odds. He was also teaching, so he was very busy. So busy, in fact, that Hillary found his campaign in disarray.

Headquarters was an old house on College Avenue

in Fayetteville. Bill Clinton was driving around the district meeting voters every day. But there was no coordinated plan. He would talk with people and collect their business cards. Or he would just write their names on scraps of paper, which he would then shove into his pocket. When he got back to campaign headquarters, he would empty his pockets into a growing pile on a table. It was not an organized effort. Until Hillary arrived.[9]

She "sat right down and went to work," said Ann Henderson, an old friend. "We didn't really have a campaign manager until she came along. Then we did."[10]

Hillary put her organizational skills to work. She even recruited her family to come down from Park Ridge and help. Her father—a lifelong Republican—crossed party lines and answered the phones at headquarters. Hillary's brothers Tony and Hugh hung Clinton campaign posters all over the district.[11]

Clinton made a strong showing on election day, but even with the help of the Rodham family he didn't win. Afterwards he went back to teaching at the University of Arkansas, where Hillary was now also a law professor. There would be plenty more campaigns in the future. For now they both settled into teaching.

Hillary began to adjust to life in a small college town, and found that she liked it. After all, Bill Clinton's friends were going all out to make her feel welcome. He had enlisted their help.

The new first lady speaks to a crowd of admirers who greeted her at
the Little Rock airport in March 1993.

"We knew that Hillary was coming down to sort of check things out," business professor Ann Henry told the *Washington Post.* "Since she was so special to Bill—and he wanted her to love it here—we did everything we could to make sure she realized she could have a wonderful, full life in Arkansas."[12]

There weren't a lot of movers and shakers in Clinton's home state. It wasn't a center of national politics. But there were good people, and it was a fine place to live. Clinton made sure that Hillary saw the best of what the area had to offer.

"He wanted her to like Arkansas, he wanted her to like Fayetteville, he was crazy about her, and he wanted to marry her," said another friend, Margaret Whillock. "It was a great time in our lives. There was a lot of warmth, a lot of camaraderie. Bill loved to tell these Arkansas stories—we all did—and we used to eat a lot, sitting around on the floor of my living room, eating after ball games and talking till all hours. It was a good place to live, a good time."[13]

Clinton's plan worked. The community welcomed Hillary, and she embraced the community.

"I loved Fayetteville," Hillary said. "I loved the university. I loved the law school. I loved my colleagues. I made some of the best friends I ever had in my life."[14]

Still, it was a trade-off. Much as she liked Arkansas, Hillary must sometimes have wondered about the opportunities she was missing. A year later, she was still deciding if it was the place for her. Obviously Bill Clinton was the reason she was there. It was time for Hillary to make up her mind about him. So she took a vacation. She went back to Park Ridge. Then she went east to New York, Boston, and Washington, D.C., to visit friends.

When she flew back to Little Rock, Clinton picked her up at the airport. He told her he had a surprise. Instead of taking her straight home, he drove to a small brick house near the university campus.

"I bought that house you liked," he told Hillary. "So you'd better marry me, because I don't want to live there alone."[15]

Hillary had admired the house one day and noticed that it was for sale. That was all Bill Clinton needed. He bought it for $21,000, then made his pitch. Hillary accepted his proposal. They were married on October 11, 1975.

The wedding took place in the house Clinton had bought. With her mother's help, Hillary bought her wedding dress at the last minute at a department store in Fayetteville. It was a small ceremony. Only close friends and family attended. Hugh and Tony Rodham, both students at the University of Arkansas, were there. The groom was 29, the bride was 27.

"It was the simplest ceremony possible, but also the most beautiful," Dorothy Rodham said later. "To see these two brilliant students loaded with diplomas, which

Hillary Rodham and Bill Clinton were married October 11, 1975, in a simple ceremony in the small house Clinton bought as a surprise for Hillary. The photo is as it appeared in the *Arkansas Democrat.* Hillary kept her last name.

could have brought them all the luxury and money in the world, there in Arkansas, in that modest house, because they had dreams of realizing their ideals. It was so moving."[16]

A reception was held the next day at a friend's house. There were about 300 guests. Many were old friends from Park Ridge, Wellesley, Yale, and Washington; some were new friends from Fayetteville and local political figures. They all came to help Hillary and Bill celebrate their new start together.

The two had been on the same path for several years. Now it was official. Hillary agreed to share her future with Bill Clinton. But she kept her own name.

The "Lady Lawyer"

Hillary and Bill were busy after the wedding. Both were teaching at the University of Arkansas and fully involved in campus life. There wasn't time for a honeymoon, they said.

Dorothy Rodham wouldn't hear of it. She arranged a trip to Acapulco. The whole family went—the new husband and wife, her brothers and her parents. They even stayed in the same hotel. Hugh Rodham told *People* magazine, "We had a marvelous time."[1]

When they returned to Fayetteville, Hillary and Bill took on the life of a young married couple in a small town. Two well-educated law professors, they made a good team. They had many friends and a happy life.

At least one friend had hoped that it would turn out differently between Hillary and Bill. Betsey Wright was another McGovern campaign worker whom they had met in Texas in 1972. Wright later worked on Clinton's campaigns, including his 1992 presidential victory, but in the mid-1970s, he wasn't the candidate she hoped for. She told *Vanity Fair:* "I was disappointed when they married. I had images in my mind that she could be the first woman president."[2]

Hillary for president? Why not? There was no law against married women seeking public office. But in the mid-1970s, even unmarried women rarely ran. And if a woman married a man in politics, it was assumed that she would support his career. She could forget about her own ambitions.

So Betsey Wright figured that Hillary's potential as a candidate was lost when she got married. Other friends had also imagined her winning elections.

"I expected her to hold some kind of political office," said her friend Kris Rogers. "I wouldn't . . . say president, but I remember we clearly thought she'd probably at least be a senator. She was an effective communicator, she was articulate, she was willing to stand up and speak out and not just shrink to the sidelines."[3]

Hillary never did shrink. Fayetteville *was* the sidelines, however. There was just not a lot of political activity there. At Wellesley, at Yale, and in Washington, people had demanded change. There were constant meetings and frequent demonstrations. Arkansas was much quieter. But neither her location nor her marriage would stand in the way of Hillary's activism.

She created her own opportunities. Again, she helped people who found themselves in the role of underdog. She set up a legal services clinic in Fayetteville that offered help to people who couldn't afford to pay lawyers. She also established a rape crisis center. These causes were important to her, and to the people she was helping. But sometimes it was an uphill climb.

People in Arkansas were not accustomed to a woman like Hillary Rodham. She was challenging some basic assumptions. She kept her maiden name after she was married. That was unusual. Just by working, she broke a long-standing rule. Many people still expected women to stay home and raise children. Hillary's friend Diane Blair, a political science professor at the University of Arkansas, remembers those days.

"As two of the few female faculty members, we were acutely aware of the suspicion with which many of the old-timers still regarded women. . . . Hillary's position as one of northwest Arkansas's few 'lady lawyers' (as one local judge persistently and publicly described her) made her even more visible and controversial."[4]

Hillary and Diane Blair had both been born and educated elsewhere. Outsiders, they developed a close friendship. They often played tennis and went for brisk walks together. They talked about the frustrations they shared. During the 1960s they had seen many rapid changes. But the South was slow to change. Their friendship helped them be patient.

"It was not easy being a feminist in Arkansas in the 1970s, and Hillary and I were very glad to have each other for advice, comfort, and comic relief,"[5] according to Blair.

Even with the challenges, Hillary liked Fayetteville. She and Bill Clinton were young and in love. They had close friendships with other couples. As Hillary told a reporter:

"We had a wonderful life there. The pace of life was so much slower, so much more open to long conversations with friends and dinners that went on for hours, where you talked about everything that was going on in your life and in the world."[6]

They lived at that relaxed pace for less than one year. In the spring of 1976, Bill Clinton launched his second run for office. This time he was elected attorney general of Arkansas. Bill and Hillary left Fayetteville and moved to the state capital of Little Rock.

There Hillary joined the Rose Law Firm in 1977. It was among the biggest and best-known firms in the state. She was one of the first women to work in a major Arkansas law firm.[7] Any doubts as to whether Hillary could successfully practice law were soon dispelled. One attorney she worked with was William R. Wilson, Jr.

Hillary was "unusually bright . . . wise, incisive," he said. As he put it, she knew how to "appeal to your mind

Hillary and Bill sing at a church service in Little Rock in 1978. Her Methodist faith is an important part of Hillary's life.

and your heart at the same time."[8] Her talent for connecting with all sorts of people was again proving a valuable asset.

"Hillary has a remarkable ability to speak in plain language, without being condescending," said Wilson. "She gets to the heart of the matter, takes a large amount of material and reduces it down to its lowest common denominator about as fast as anybody I've ever seen. And she can talk about it all in non-legal language."[9]

She remained active in politics, too. President Jimmy Carter's staff was impressed with her work in a presidential primary in 1976. The next year Carter appointed Hillary to the board of directors of the Legal Services Corporation, an agency that provides federal funds to legal-aid clinics around the country. It's also based in Washington. Serving on the board reconnected Hillary to the policy-makers in the nation's capital.[10]

While Hillary established her reputation as a lawyer, her husband was making news as the attorney general of Arkansas. As the state's chief law enforcement officer, he took many steps that would benefit average citizens. He fought for consumer rights, and developed a reputation as a populist, one who represented the common people.[11]

The press appreciated Bill Clinton's activism. One newspaper reported that "his record as attorney general has been studded with examples of hard work, consumer concerns, and a generally aggressive stance that has led him into a variety of situations with seeming zest."[12] The paper also wondered when Clinton would seek higher office.

It didn't take long. In 1978, Bill Clinton decided to run for governor of Arkansas. A campaign statement he made then outlined his beliefs. His outlook was remarkably close to Hillary's philosophy of public service.

"All my life, I've wanted to be involved with people and help them with their problems," said Clinton. "I've been very interested in all kinds of people. Politics has just given me a way to pursue my interest and my concern on a large scale. I've given it all the energy and spirit I can muster. I've tried to bring out the best in people through politics. And I've really been very happy doing it."[13]

Many politicians dislike campaigning. Clinton thrived on it. He enjoyed meeting people, and talking with them about their concerns. Arkansas voters responded well to the tireless young candidate. He won the primary handily, then went on to defeat his Republican opponent by almost two votes to one. It was a dream come true. He and Hillary moved into the governor's mansion.

At 32, Bill Clinton was the nation's youngest governor. He was full of energy and new ideas. He chose energetic young people for many key positions on his staff. Through appointments, he added many women and minorities to state boards and commissions.

By the second year of his term, there was another addition coming to his own family. In 1979, Hillary announced that she was pregnant. She continued her work at the Rose Law Firm through much of her pregnancy. Then, on February 27, 1980, Hillary gave birth to a healthy baby girl. They called her Chelsea. The origin of her name dated from the previous year, when Hillary and Bill were visiting London. As Hillary explained to *Newsweek:* "It was this glorious morning. We were going to brunch and we were walking through Chelsea, you know, the flowerpots were out and everything. And Bill started singing "It's a Chelsea morning." It was a song by 1960s folk singer Judy Collins.[14]

Both Bill and Hillary had led full, busy lives before Chelsea was born. Parenthood demanded a new level of devotion. Hillary had grown up in a supportive household. She knew how important her parents were to her development. Now she wanted to provide a nurturing environment for her own daughter. It was not easy juggling all her responsibilities, but Hillary put motherhood first.

"I have tried very hard to put my obligation to my daughter ahead of everything," she said later. "And one of the things I have tried to do is make sure she not only had the support she needed but the time she needed."[15]

Becoming a parent had a big effect on her husband too. Bill Clinton, Hillary said, was "amazed by

Hillary and her daughter Chelsea—named after a 1960s folk song—pose in 1984. Chelsea is four years old in this picture.

fatherhood." Chelsea's arrival made 1980 a joyous year for the two of them. But the year also held a major disappointment.

There was an election in the fall. Clinton had worked hard and started many innovative programs during his first term.[16] But it wasn't enough for the people of Arkansas. Clinton lost his first re-election bid, to Republican Frank White.

One term was not enough to do everything he wanted. Bill Clinton had spent most of his life creating his political foundation. He hoped to build upon it for many years to come. But it had already crumbled before his eyes. Hillary would help him piece it back together.

8

The Campaign Trail

Hillary's friend Diane Blair remembers the day after Bill Clinton lost the Arkansas governorship in 1980. She and her husband Jim went to lunch with Hillary and Bill. The defeated Clinton was half-laughing, half-crying at a country and western tune on the restaurant jukebox. The song was called, "I Feel So Bad I Don't Know Whether to Kill Myself or Go Bowling."[1]

He really *did* feel bad. At age 34, Clinton had achieved his dream, then lost it. He was unsure what his next step should be. He soon went to work for a private law firm, but his heart was not in it.[2]

Clinton was depressed, and it took several months for him to shake it off. Some have suggested that there may have been trouble in Hillary and Bill's marriage

Bill Clinton and Hillary keep a watchful eye on election returns on the night of his first bid to be re-elected as governor of Arkansas in 1980. Clinton lost, and was crushed by the defeat.

during this time. There were rumors that he was having an affair with another woman.[3]

Years later, Bill Clinton would be forced to confront these reports. During the 1992 presidential campaign he admitted "causing pain" in his marriage. But he was never more definite than that. Hillary was also questioned about the rumors. *Newsweek's* Eleanor Clift asked her for specific examples of "rocky periods in your marriage." Hillary responded: "I don't think that is anybody else's concern. What is important to us is that we have always dealt with each other. We haven't run away, or walked away. We've been willing to work through all kinds of problems."[4]

The biggest problem facing them in 1980 was Clinton's sudden aimlessness. Gradually, he came out of his depression. When he did, he set his sights on the governor's mansion once again. Throughout 1981, he talked with voters everywhere he went. In February of 1982 he declared himself a candidate for the election that fall. Hillary took a leave of absence from the Rose Law Firm. She would help her husband win his job back.

For this campaign, Hillary made some practical changes. They were small things, but they would help make the difference with voters. One issue was her name. People did not understand why she still called herself Hillary Rodham. The women's movement had not exactly swept through the South. Almost every

Hillary gives her account of why her husband's campaign for governor in 1980 was unsuccessful. When Clinton decided to run again, she campaigned with him, going now by the name of Mrs. Bill Clinton.

married woman in Arkansas went by her husband's last name.

She had kept her maiden name after she was married because it was "important to me that I be judged on my merits, and that Bill be judged on his merits," Hillary told a reporter.[5] Keeping her name was a way of keeping her own identity. She didn't expect it to become a big issue among voters. But it had. Many of her husband's supporters asked her to think about calling herself Hillary Clinton. Bill never did, she said.

"I joked one time that probably the only man in Arkansas who didn't ask me to change my name was my husband—who said, 'This is your decision, and you do exactly what you want.' And so I did. I just decided that it was not an issue that was that big to me when it came right down to it."[6]

Her name couldn't make any difference in how Clinton governed, but she responded to the pressure. She announced that she would still practice law as Hillary Rodham, but in appearances as the candidate's wife, she would be known as Mrs. Bill Clinton.[7]

She also began paying more attention to her appearance. She traded in her thick glasses for some contact lenses. Hillary had tried to wear contacts in high school, but the hard lenses irritated her eyes. By 1982, there were soft lenses that she could wear comfortably. She got her hair cut in a more stylish way. Then she went out campaigning.

She was the same person she had always been—bright, friendly, and engaging. But the small changes seemed to make a big difference in how people viewed Hillary.

"Mrs. Clinton is almost certainly the best speaker among the politicians' wives, probably the only one who can fully engage an audience on her own merits, rather than just as someone's wife," the *Arkansas Gazette* noted. "The name change indicates that she's softening her image a bit . . . and succeeding, apparently. She has become a good hand-shaking campaigner in the traditional Arkansas style."[8]

Hillary became more visible than before, more of a public partner with her husband. The voters seemed to approve. Clinton won back the governor's post in 1982. Hillary, Bill, and Chelsea triumphantly moved into the mansion in Little Rock again. This time Governor Clinton would listen more closely to the voters. He was determined to do the very best job he could.

Clinton knew he had to boost the state's economy. The best way to do this would be to provide young people with strong basic skills. The schools had to do a better job of preparing students for the future. Improving the education system in Arkansas became Clinton's top priority.

He formed an Education Standards Committee. This group would study the problem and make

After two years out of the Arkansas governor's mansion, Hillary and Bill moved back in. Here Hillary carries a plant in through the front entrance.

recommendations to the Arkansas legislature. In 1983, Clinton appointed Hillary to head the committee.

"This guarantees that I will have a person who is closer to me than anyone else overseeing a project that is more important to me than anything else," said Clinton. "I don't know if it's a politically wise move, but it's the right thing to do."[9]

It was a tough job. Hillary toured Arkansas for months. She visited all of the state's 75 counties. Everywhere she went she discussed with people how the schools could be improved. She listened closely. And when she talked, people were impressed. In Pulaski County, she told the P.T.A.: "We expect nothing but the best from our athletes: discipline, teamwork, standards. I wish we could translate the same expectations and standards we have for athletics into the classroom. I wish we could give teachers the same praise and support for teaching children to read as we do those who teach them to throw a ball through a hoop."[10]

Finally, the committee made its recommendations. The plan included several tax increases. The most controversial part of the package was a competency test for teachers. Teachers hated that idea. Some of them began hissing at Hillary when she appeared in public. One educator said Hillary was "lower than a snake's belly."[11]

It was not fun being unpopular. The plan was strong medicine. But the governor and his wife and other

Hillary models her second inaugural gown inside the Arkansas governor's mansion in 1983. Bill Clinton would be re-elected five times in the 1980s. Hillary's career as a lawyer took off, too.

lawmakers in the state believed it was what Arkansas needed. In the end the legislature passed the package. Soon Bill Clinton was nationally recognized as an education reformer. In his home state he became the most popular governor ever. He won every election he entered during the 1980s, and served a record five terms.

Hillary's career also took off during the 1980s. She was appointed to the board of three large corporations: Wal-Mart; TCBY Enterprises; and Lafarge. She had worked as a staff attorney for the Children's Defense Fund in the 1970s, and in 1986, she became the agency's chairperson. In 1987, Hillary was named chair of the American Bar Association's Commission on Women in the Profession. In 1988 and 1991, she was ranked among the top 100 most influential lawyers in America by *The National Law Journal.* She also became the chief breadwinner in the family. The most Bill Clinton earned as governor was $35,000 per year. Hillary, meanwhile, was bringing home more than $200,000 annually.

By 1987, Bill Clinton was considering a run for the presidency. He felt that Arkansas had made good progress under his leadership. Now he wanted to serve his country. But Bill and Hillary decided that a presidential campaign would be too hard on Chelsea, then age 7. So he skipped the 1988 campaign.

In 1991, Bill Clinton declared himself a candidate for the highest office in the land. Chelsea was 11 and better prepared to handle the media spotlight that came with a national campaign. Clinton felt ready, too. He had learned a great deal while governing Arkansas. He and Hillary both saw many problems that needed to be addressed on a national level. He focused especially on the economy and on education.

The 1992 presidential campaign was a long ordeal for both Hillary and Bill. Clinton was repeatedly attacked by opponents and the press. He was accused of dodging the draft and smoking marijuana. Again, there were rumors that Bill Clinton had cheated on Hillary. The low point came in January, just before the start of the primaries. A woman named Gennifer Flowers claimed to have carried on a 12-year affair with Bill Clinton.

The story first appeared in the *Star,* one of the supermarket tabloids that specializes in false, ridiculous stories. Hillary was campaigning in Atlanta when the story hit.

"It's not true," she said. "I just don't believe any of that. All of these people, including that woman, have denied this many, many times. I'm not going to speculate on her motives. We know she was paid."[12]

Most people realize that stories in supermarket tabloids are not to be believed. But the nation's mainstream press picked up the story and ran it anyway. The story was reported in many newspapers and TV newscasts. Clinton's campaign advisors felt that he had

Hillary jokes with photographers in the governor's mansion in 1988. Bill Clinton had considered running for president that year. But he and Hillary decided that a national campaign would be too rough on Chelsea.

to respond to the charges, and in a big way. They decided that Bill and Hillary should appear on the CBS-TV show "60 Minutes."

The program was broadcast on January 26, 1992, immediately following the Super Bowl. Millions of Americans watched the candidate and his wife state their case.

"I have acknowledged wrongdoing, I have acknowledged causing pain in my marriage," Clinton said during the interview. But he refused to go any further. Interviewer Steve Kroft pressed for more details. Hillary cut in: "There isn't a person watching this who would feel comfortable sitting on this couch, detailing everything that ever went on in their life or their marriage. And I think it's real dangerous in this country if we don't have some zone of privacy for everybody. I mean, I think that is absolutely critical."

Kroft replied: "I. . ., I. . ., I couldn't agree with you more."[13]

A few minutes later, Hillary closed the book on the issue. "You know, I'm not sitting here, some little woman standing by my man like Tammy Wynette," she said. "I'm sitting here because I love him and I respect him and I honor what he's been through and what we've been through together. And you know, if that's not enough for people, then heck, don't vote for him."[14]

Hillary's choice of words wasn't fully appreciated by Tammy Wynette, the country singer whose biggest hit was "Stand By Your Man." But many voters and the national media were impressed.

Three weeks later, the primary was held in New Hampshire. A lot of mud had been slung. Many figured Clinton's candidacy was finished. But he came in second behind Paul Tsongas. The surprisingly strong showing put him on the comeback trail. With Hillary's help, Bill Clinton was rolling toward the presidential nomination.

9

At the Center of the Storm

It's a long and bumpy road to the White House. The Clinton campaign faced more obstacles after the "60 Minutes" segment, and Hillary was often at the center of the action. One episode seemed to sum up the sort of campaign it was.

Former California Governor Jerry Brown was one of Bill Clinton's opponents for the Democratic nomination. He suggested that Bill and Hillary improperly used each other's connections in business and government. Brown said the that Rose Law Firm profited unfairly from business with the state of Arkansas. Hillary responded to his charges with a little bit of sarcasm. It was unlike her, and she probably soon regretted it.

"I suppose I could have stayed home and baked

cookies and had teas," Hillary said. "But what I decided to do was pursue my profession, which I entered before my husband was in public life."[1]

The quote was widely reported in the news media. By itself, the statement made it seem as if Hillary was criticizing women who dedicated themselves to motherhood, rather than a career. But most people did not hear everything she said that day. She followed up: "The work that I have done . . . has been aimed . . . to assure that women can make the choices . . . whether it's full-time career, full-time motherhood, or some combination,"[2] she said.

Hillary was discovering that she was a symbol. Many people still had mixed feelings about strong women. When they saw her on TV, saying something that seemed to ridicule women who didn't work, it angered them. Hillary was perplexed. People were judging her based on a 20-second, out-of-context sound bite. She was being attacked by people who didn't know her, or what she believed.

When she was invited to speak once again to the graduates at Wellesley College's commencement, Hillary tried to explain her position to the women in the audience.

"You may choose to be a corporate executive or a rocket scientist," she said. "You may run for public office, or you may stay at home with your children. You can now make any or all of these choices, and they can be the work of your life."[3]

Her life's work was helping children, she told the Wellesley graduates. She pursued that work as an attorney, and she didn't like having to defend her life as a professional. What mattered was that women should have the option to pursue their goals in their professional lives, as well as their personal lives.

"You can do it making policies or making cookies," she said.

The cookies quote had provoked a strong reaction. Obviously, there was some confusion about having a woman involved in national politics. People were learning more about Hillary. But they still weren't sure what the proper role of the candidate's wife was in the 1990s.

Both Hillary and Bill had been saying that a vote for Clinton was "a two-for-one." The line had worked well during campaigns in Arkansas. But now it seemed to raise unsettling questions. Who was running for president, after all, Bill Clinton or his wife? If their marriage was an equal partnership, who then would be making the decisions if Clinton was elected?

It was a conflict many adults felt in their own lives. Since the beginning of the women's movement, millons of American women had entered the work force. Throughout the 1970s and 1980s, women became empowered; they had their own paychecks that rewarded their own individual abilities. Likewise, as women grew familiar with the pressures of the workplace, many of their husbands learned to share in the duties of running a household.

Working couples were not a new phenomenon. Yet the idea of a working couple in the White House frightened people. Some did not like the idea of a president with a wife who might help him make decisions. Others figured it would be a good thing for the nation's leader to have a smart and capable partner. There was no consensus. But even as the debate raged, Clinton locked up the Democratic nomination in the summer of 1992.

Meanwhile, Hillary became less of a presence. She tried not to make controversial statements. She poked fun at herself by entering a cookie-baking contest with First Lady Barbara Bush. Hillary won, according to a poll of those who tried the two recipes. She also changed her look, as she had many times before.

She dealt with the headband issue. For some reason, people were bothered by the headbands Hillary often wore to keep her hair in place. Some saw her as a stuck-up yuppie lawyer when she wore a headband. She made it a non-issue by having her hair cut shorter. She also picked out a stylish new wardrobe. In interviews she became quieter. Suddenly she was a little more first lady-like.

If small adjustments would help win the campaign,

Hillary in Washington, D.C., during the 1992 campaign. She is wearing one of the headbands that became a source of controversy.

Hillary could make them. She had done so before. The opposition would not let her adjust her image so easily, however. As a progressive, professional woman in national politics, Hillary represented change—a kind of change that some people still resisted. The Republican convention in July 1992 turned into a Hillary-bashing party.

"Hillary pounds the piano so hard that Bill can't be heard," said former President Richard Nixon. "You want a wife who's intelligent, but not too intelligent."[4]

Nixon was from a bygone era. In his day, girls were trained and women were expected to be submissive. But the world had changed. By the 1990s many women were more active in determining their own fate.

The former president was not the only one who tried to put a negative spin on Hillary's stature as a bright, successful woman. Marilyn Quayle, wife of the vice president and also a lawyer, gave a speech in which she said that "most women do not wish to be liberated from their essential natures as women."[5] Others pointed to Hillary's legal writings from the 1970s and accused her of being "anti-family."

She did indeed argue in her writings that adolescents ought to have a say in major decisions in their lives. But she also maintained that government should be very careful about intruding in family relationships. As one legal scholar wrote in *The Wall Street Journal:* "The charge that she is anti-family is a distortion without basis in her writings."[6]

Some observers said that the debate was more about the changing role of women than about Hillary herself.

"It's not her," said feminist Gloria Steinem. "It's her and him. She's pioneering in public an issue that is at least as important in the long term as any of the issues considered political in the conventional sense, and that is an equal relationship between a man and a woman."[7]

The opposition hoped that by drawing attention to Hillary, they could scare voters away from Bill Clinton. But the strategy soon backfired. The press seemed to decide that maybe Hillary wasn't so bad. Like millions of American women, she was trying to juggle her family and a career, and was doing it well. How could having an intelligent, accomplished wife hurt a candidate? It began to occur to people that Hillary might actually be her husband's greatest asset.

Support for the Clinton candidacy grew through the summer of 1992. By fall, President George Bush was losing his lead. He would not regain it and independent Texas billionaire Ross Perot never gained major support. On November 3, 1992, the American public chose Bill Clinton as president of the United States.

10

Introducing President and Mrs. Clinton

At noon on January 20, 1993, the Clintons stood on the west front of the United States Capitol. Hillary held a King James Bible under her husband's left hand. The Bible had been given to Bill Clinton by his grandmother. It was open to the New Testament, Galatians 6:8. The passage read: "*For he that soweth to his flesh shall of the flesh reap corruption; but he that soweth to the Spirit shall of the Spirit reap life everlasting.*"

Bill Clinton raised his right hand. He was about to become the 42nd president of the United States. The crowd of onlookers hushed. They stretched from the white stone steps of the flag-draped Capitol down the Mall to the Washington Monument. At 250,000, it was the largest inauguration gathering in U.S. history. Millions more watched on television.[1]

It was a windless, cloudless day. The temperature was in the low 40s. Birds floated quietly in the reflecting pool in front of the Lincoln Memorial. On the podium, William H. Rehnquist, Chief Justice of the Supreme Court, read the short oath. Clinton repeated after him: "I, William Jefferson Clinton, do solemnly swear that I will faithfully execute the office of the president of the United States, and will to the best of my ability preserve, protect, and defend the Constitution of the United States, so help me God."[2]

With those words the torch was passed. George Bush and his wife Barbara stepped down. In the bright, crisp sunshine of winter, Bill and Hillary Clinton took their place as the nation's first couple.

The inauguration ceremony completed a slow transition that had begun long before. In places like Hope and Park Ridge, at Georgetown, Oxford, Wellesley, Yale, and in Little Rock, a younger generation had prepared for this moment. It was their turn now. The Clintons had been leaders of their generation. Now they were the new leaders of America. Hillary Rodham Clinton—strong, visible, and involved—was a new kind of first lady.

Before she took on her new role, Hillary read biographies of all the women who had been first ladies before her. She learned that there had been powerful presidential wives in the past. Eleanor Roosevelt acted as the eyes and ears of her invalid husband. She was also an activist with her own causes. And she influenced her husband's thinking on the most important issues of the day.

Other first ladies were remembered more for their style. Dolley Madison was famous for her Wednesday-night receptions and the French pastries she served at them. Mamie Eisenhower was best known for being in the pink. She had pink furniture and pink sheets on her bed. She wrote notes on pink paper, and liked pink flowers. She wore a pink ribbon in her hair, pink shoes on her feet, and pink lipstick.[3]

Mamie Eisenhower's successor, Jacqueline Kennedy, made a point of supporting the arts. Lady Bird Johnson promoted beautification of the landscape, and Rosalynn Carter attended cabinet meetings. In the 1980s, Nancy Reagan was noteworthy for her lavish evening gowns and her "Just Say No" anti-drug campaign. Barbara Bush made literacy her issue, and wrote a best-selling book from her dog's point of view.

All of these women had power, but it was always an extension of their husbands' power. By 1993, many people were ready for a first lady who reflected a new reality in American society. Women had gained a bigger share of power in the workplace, in their marriages, and in society overall.

Hillary embodied that change. She was among the first female students at Yale Law School. She had been the first woman in a traditional old law firm in the

Hillary and Chelsea at one of Chelsea's soccer matches in Little Rock in 1987. Although she has an extremely busy schedule, Hillary makes sure she has time to spend with her daughter.

South. She knew what it was like to accommodate the demands of her job and the needs of her family. Now she was the first lady of the land. As Hillary told a national TV audience a few nights before the inauguration: "What is being played out in the homes of America is now being played out in the White House."[4]

The playing out began on inauguration day. After Clinton was sworn in, poet Maya Angelou recited "On the Pulse of Morning." It was a poem of hope that she wrote for the occasion. Then the Clintons rode in a bulletproof limousine toward their new home. A few blocks from the White House, they got out of the car and strolled down Pennsylvania Avenue. Secret Service agents carefully watched the cheering crowds along the street.

The new president and his wife of 16 years walked about 10 feet apart, waving to the excited, flag-waving crowds. Occasionally, they came together and held hands. Unlike the Carters, Reagans, and Bushes, who held hands all the way down the avenue, the Clintons would touch briefly, then separate, and each wave to the crowd on a different side of the street.[5]

When they got to the White House, the Clintons watched for several hours as an enthusiastic parade marched by their viewing stand. Inside the iron gates, moving vans with Arkansas license plates were unloading. The house at 1600 Pennsylvania Avenue would be their home for at least the next four years.

That night the new first couple made appearances at many of the inaugural balls around the city. Everyone wanted to see them. Politicians, celebrities and cameramen jostled for a glimpse of the new president and his wife. Hillary wore a lavender gown, loaded with crystal beads. It was from one of her favorite dressmakers back in Little Rock.

The Clintons visited as many of the inaugural balls as they could, then returned to the White House at about 3 A.M. They got up early the next day and went to work, welcoming thousands of visitors and well-wishers.

One of the first things Hillary did as she settled into her new home was to ban smoking. Next, she added more vegetables to the menu. Then she broke with tradition and set up her office in a small, sunny room in the West Wing, near the Oval Office.

All previous first ladies had operated out of the East Wing, far from the president. Unlike them, however, Hillary had an official policy-making job. The president had appointed her head of the Task Force on National Health Reform. Overseeing the effort to reform the nation's health-care system was probably the most difficult task in the administration. The situation was very similar to when Hillary had chaired the Education Standards Committee in Arkansas. But the stakes were much higher.

As she told *Parade* in 1993: "My husband believes it is worth any risk to create a new health-care system for this country. I don't think he believes it's worth being president if he can't do that. He feels that strongly about it. Health-care reform is one of his two chief goals. The other, obviously, is creating new jobs that will bring about rising incomes again. That's the primary goal. But creating a new health-care system goes hand-in-hand with that. Because health-care costs are undermining our economic prosperity."[6]

It was a big challenge. But Hillary was aiming even higher.

11

The Hillary Style

Early in the Clinton presidency the nation was hungry for information about the new first lady. The news media obliged. Hillary's image flickered across millions of TV screens every day. Her face was on the front pages of countless newspapers and magazines. Still, many people didn't really know who she was.

It's not easy to know Hillary. She is a very private person. She did give several interviews early in 1993, however. It was as if she had decided it was time to get acquainted with the American people. From these interviews the press began to draw a picture of the new first lady. As one magazine writer mused: "Americans are finally getting clued in on what Arkansans easily recognize: Hillary Clinton is virtually a co-president with her own style and influence."[1]

For the first lady to be labeled "co-president" was unthinkable until Hillary came along. More than her style, however, it was her substance that allowed her to pull it off. Like other top-notch lawyers, she's efficient and to the point. Meetings with Hillary move along briskly. She is known for her blunt, businesslike manner. Most importantly, she gets things done. She does not waste time with people who are unprepared. She expects the best, and sometimes that surprises people.

"She is such a perfectionist—hard on herself, hard on others," observed one reporter.[2] Someone who worked for the Clintons for several years said Hillary can at times be impatient with others:

> She doesn't come from a rich family, she wasn't really snobby that way, [but] she expects so much out of people—she'd yell at a waitress, somebody driving her around [in] taxicabs . . . there's no room for mistakes or anything in her mind. She does look down at people, she feels like she's so brilliant, everybody should have as much sense as she does.[3]

It's true that she is focused. Hillary can be so intense that people sometimes wonder if she's a workaholic with no sense of humor. Yet she does have a rowdy side, according to Maggie Williams, her chief of staff.[4]

Among insiders on the 1992 campaign, she was known for pulling pranks and telling jokes. Her closest friends have seen her do funny impersonations of various people she has met—high school boyfriends and college professors, for instance. She does an especially good one of a legal client upset at finding a rodent in a can of food.[5] She appreciates humor in others, too. When she allows herself, she opens wide and unleashes a loud, rollicking belly laugh.

Hillary is also a tomboy, according to writer Walter Shapiro.[6] She's been a serious fan of the Chicago Cubs since childhood, when her father took her to see the team play. In 1993, she was scheduled to throw out the first baseball on opening day at Wrigley Field. She prepared by making her brothers play catch with her, so that she wouldn't "throw like a girl."[7]

More than anything, Hillary likes to spend time with her teenage daughter, Chelsea. Even during the hectic 1992 campaign, she would often fly back to Little Rock and spend a day or two with Chelsea. They would watch movies, bake cookies, or just hang out together.

Like many American women today, Hillary has several roles—mother, wife, feminist, and lawyer, to name a few. It's a sign of the changing times that she was given something that none of her predecessors in the White House ever had—an official job.

When she took on the task of fixing America's nearly $1 trillion health-care system, Hillary knew it would be her biggest political and professional challenge yet. There were plenty of people who had something to say about it. She had dozens of meetings with members of

Congress. She visited hospitals, factories, and schools. She ran hearings. She was getting up to speed fast.

Then on March 19, 1993, she dropped everything. Her father, Hugh, had suffered a stroke at the age of 82. Hillary and Chelsea flew to Little Rock to be at his side. They arrived in time to say good-bye. "When we got there, for the first couple of days he knew we were there, and it was wonderful," Hillary said.[8]

Hugh Rodham was slipping away, however. Hillary and Chelsea stayed at his bedside for two weeks. This was when Hillary was scheduled to throw out the first ball at the Cubs' opener. She decided she couldn't go through with it. She kept a speaking engagement at the University of Texas, though, and her comments there told of the issues that weighed on her mind.

"When does life start?" she asked. "When does life end? Who makes those decisions? How do we dare to impinge upon these areas of such delicate, difficult questions?"[9]

Hugh Rodham died the next night. He was buried in Scranton, Pennsylvania, where he had grown up. A few weeks later Hillary recalled one of the first lessons she learned from her father. She told a reporter from *The New York Times:* "He used to say all the time, 'I will always love you but I won't always like what you do.' And you know, as a child I would come up with 900 hypotheses. It would always end with something like,

'Well, you mean, if I murdered somebody and was in jail and you came to see me, you would still love me?'

And he would say, 'Absolutely! I will always love you, but I would be deeply disappointed and I would not like what you did, because it would have been wrong.' "[10]

That message was a key to her development, Hillary said. "It was so simplistic, but it was so helpful to me, because, I mean, it gave me the basis of unconditional love that I think every child deserves to have—and one of our problems is that too many of our children don't have that—but it also gave me from the very beginning a set of values based on what I did."[11]

Her family's love was the cornerstone for Hillary. On that and her Methodist faith she built the foundation of her personal and professional lives, as well as her political activism. She is still convinced that the first step to living well is to love and respect yourself.

"The very core of what I believe is this concept of individual worth, which I think flows from all of us, being creatures of God, and being imbued with a spirit. . . . If you break down the Golden Rule, or if you take Christ's commandment—Love they neighbor as thyself—there is an underlying assumption that you will value yourself, that you will be a responsible being who will live by certain behaviors that enable you to have self-respect, because then, out of that self-respect comes the capacity for you to respect and care for other people."[12]

Love, self-respect, and caring for other people are unusual themes for someone in political life. But Hillary seems to be trying to change the old ways of politics-as-usual. She brings a woman's perspective to what has been the rough-and-tumble man's game of national politics. Already, she has used her position to bring attention to a different kind of "politics of meaning."

As articulated by editor and writer Michael Lerner, the politics of meaning would address human needs more directly. It would be less rewarding of selfishness, and would promote more caring and cooperation in our daily lives.[13] It would be more attentive to ethical, spiritual, and psychological needs.

It seems to some people that these are important needs that are not being met in our society. To others, talk of a new politics of meaning is ridiculous. Critics say it's just not possible. Hillary has been told before that her dreams can't be reached. Yet now NASA sends women astronauts into space, and there are women lawyers and doctors, and even women Supreme Court justices. Bill Clinton added a second woman to the Supreme Court—Ruth Bader Ginsburg—who joined Sandra Day O'Connor, a Reagan appointee. All these barriers have been overcome since Hillary was a child. Now she has her sights set on fundamentally changing the way we practice politics.

How would she begin to do that? When she was

given the job of reforming the nation's health-care system, Hillary saw within that task an even larger opportunity. It called for a mix of practicality and idealism, hard work and high hopes. As she told the *New York Times* reporter:

> I really hope that we're not just solving an economic problem, although that is crucial, and we're not just restructuring the way we deliver health care. If we could do this right, so that we restore a sense of security on this issue to all Americans, then I think from that will flow a better understanding of one another, a greater recognition of our interdependence, a willingness to help each other, to share the burden of living together.[14]

That's a tall order. America has fragmented since Hillary's youth. Many people now identify themselves primarily through membership in special interest groups or in other exclusive categories. These groups generally don't want to share the burden of living together. And not everyone thinks government should involve itself too much in helping people. Still, most agree that our society needs to change.

"There are millions of people who are worried about the same things I'm worried about," Hillary said. "I want to live in a place again where I can walk down any street without being afraid. I want to be able to take my daughter to a park at any time of the day or night in the summertime and remember what I used to be able to do when I was a little kid."[15]

She talks about people making connections in ways many no longer do. In Texas, the day before her father passed away, Hillary spoke of the need for Americans to ". . . be hopeful again . . . to see other people as they wish to be seen and to treat them as they wish to be treated, to overcome all of the obstacles we have erected around ourselves that keep us apart from one another, fearful and afraid, not willing to build the bridges necessary. . . ."[16]

Again, it was not the sort of message we've come to expect from our political leaders. Most of those in government would fear being laughed out of office if they spoke about such things. Certainly, Hillary has left herself vulnerable to criticism. Her focus on spiritual and moral issues has been called vague, radical nonsense. Yet she also has a conservative streak, and a strong, practical sense of personal responsibility.

"You just have to do the best you can with whatever challenges life sends your way," she has said. "I've believed that ever since I was a little girl. . . . I've always believed you play the hand you were dealt, and you play it as well as you can. You take every precaution you possibly can to make sure that, at the end of the day, you are glad you lived it that way, and you know that you did the best job you could do."[17]

The seeds of this kind of good citizenship are

A new kind of first lady, Hillary Rodham Clinton has the tough job of reforming the nation's health-care system. She also has a wider vision for a better America.

planted in youth. Hillary feels strongly that families need support in raising individuals to be more personally responsible.

"Most parents want to give their children the right values. They want homes that are filled with love and laughter," she has said. "We need better ways of reaching out so that families can do a better job. We need to recognize that children are shaped both by the values of their parents and the policies of their nation. You can't have one without the other and expect families to flourish."[18]

She came to Washington with big ideas and a big agenda. But throughout her life Hillary has shown that she's not afraid to take what she sees as the right risks. As the new first lady, she has seen a chance to shape history by changing the way we govern ourselves. The world is watching closely to see what Hillary can accomplish.

Her fans can subscribe to the *Hillary Clinton Quarterly*, a newsletter published in New Hampshire. Her detractors only have to turn on the radio to hear new rumors. According to *Time*, one Republican consultant considers it his job to make sure Hillary Clinton is discredited before the 1996 campaign.[19] She has learned that being a high-profile public figure means that she will be the target of such attacks. It's part of the job.

As a girl in Park Ridge, Hillary Rodham set her sights on a difficult, demanding, but worthwhile job.

While she never did become an astronaut, she has reached other heights that have called on her talents, and allowed her to serve her country. As an activist first lady, she's a symbol of American womanhood. Women's roles continue to change in the 1990s, and Hillary embodies that transition.

Through the many changes in her own life she has been true to herself. As she has grown she has integrated her personal, professional, and spiritual interests. She has also striven to fulfill her responsibility to the larger community, by dedicating herself to public service. Whatever else she ultimately accomplishes, Hillary Rodham Clinton has already proven that when you dare to try, you can begin to change the world.

Chronology

1947—Hillary Rodham is born in Chicago.

1950—Rodham family moves to Park Ridge, Illinois.

1964—Joins family in supporting Barry Goldwater for president.

1965—Enters Wellesley College.

1969—Graduates from Wellesley, is first student commencement speaker.

1969—Enters Yale Law School.

1970—Meets Marion Wright Edelman and Bill Clinton.

1972—Travels to Texas to work for McGovern presidential campaign.

1974—Appointed to House Judiciary Subcommittee investigating Watergate affair. Takes job teaching law at the University of Arkansas.

1975—Marries Bill Clinton, keeps her last name.

1977—Joins Rose Law Firm in Little Rock.

1978—Becomes first lady of Arkansas.

1980—Gives birth to daughter, Chelsea. Bill Clinton loses reelection bid.

1982—Campaigning as Hillary Rodham Clinton, helps her husband win back Arkansas governorship.

1983—Chairs Arkansas Education Standards Committee.

1988—Named one of the top 100 lawyers in the nation.

1991—Bill Clinton enters presidential race.

1993—Clinton inaugurated, Hillary becomes first lady.

Chapter Notes

Chapter 1

1. Judith Warner, *Hillary Clinton: The Inside Story* (New York: Signet, 1993), p. 15.

2. Ibid.

3. Ibid.

4. Associated Press, "Hillary Clinton Schooled in Doctrine of Methodism," *Los Angeles Times,* Dec. 5, 1992, p. B4.

Chapter 2

1. Martha Sherrill, "The Education of Hillary Clinton: Her Journey From Goldwater Girl to First Lady," *Washington Post,* Jan. 11, 1993, p. B1.

2. Ibid.

3. John A. Garraty and Peter Gay (eds.), "The United States Since World War II," *Columbia History of the World(* New York: Harper and Row, Publishers, Inc., 1972), p. 1140.

4. Sherrill, p. B1.

5. Judith Warner, *Hillary Clinton: The Inside Story* (New York: Signet, 1993), p. 16.

6. Howard G. Chua-Eoan, Nina Burleigh, and Linda Kramer, "Power Mom," *People,* Jan. 25, 1993, p. 53.

7. Sherrill, p. B1.

8. Ibid.

9. Dotson Rader, "Hillary Rodham Clinton: People Who Inspire Me," *Parade,* April 11, 1993, p. 14.

10. Warner, 1993, p. 16.

11. Sherrill, 1993, p. B1.

12. Ibid.

13. Ibid.

14. Ibid.

15. Ibid.

16. Chua-Eoan et al., p. 53.

17. Sherrill, p. B1.

18. Ibid.

19. Warner, p. 24.

20. Sherrill, p. B1.

21. Warner, p. 27.

22. Sherrill, p. B1.

23. Warner, p. 23.

Chapter 3

1. Charles F. Allen and Jonathan Portis, *The Comeback Kid: The Life and Career of Bill Clinton* (New York: Birch Lane Press, 1992,) p. 207.

2. Martha Sherrill, "The Education of Hillary Clinton," *Washington Post,* Jan. 12, 1993, p. B1.

3. Judith Warner, *Hillary Clinton, The Inside Story* (New York: Signet, 1993), p. 28.

4. Dotson Rader, "We Are All Responsible," *Parade,* April 11, 1993, p. 6.

5. Sherrill, p. B1.

6. Warner, p. 27.

7. Howard G. Chua-Eoan, Nina Burleigh, and Linda Kramer, "Power Mom," *People,* Jan. 25, 1993, p. 54.

8. Warner, p. 29.

9. Rader, p. 5.

10. Warner, p. 33.

11. Ibid, p. 37.

12. Ibid, p. 39.

13. Ibid, p. 39.

14. Ibid, p. 40.

Chapter 4

1. Judith Warner, *Hillary Clinton: The Inside Story* (New York: Signet, 1993), p. 41.

2. Charles F. Allen and Jonathan Portis, *The Comeback Kid: The Life and Career of Bill Clinton* (New York: Birch Lane Press, 1992), p. 210.

3. Warner, p. 36.

4. Ibid, p. 43.

5. Ibid.

6. Martha Sherrill, "The Rising Lawyer's Detour to Arkansas," *Washington Post*, Jan. 12, 1993, p. B 2.

7. Ibid.

8. Warner, p. 61.

9. Ibid, p. 51.

10. Ibid.

11. Ibid, p. 52.

12. Ibid, p. 46.

13. Ibid, p. 49.

14. Allen and Portis, p. 33.

15. Dotson Rader, "We Are All Responsible," *Parade*, April 11, 1993, p. 6.

Chapter 5

1. Judith Warner, *Hillary Clinton: The Inside Story* (New York: Signet, 1993), p. 47.

2. Ibid, p. 49.

3. Ibid, p. 60.

4. Charles F. Allen and Jonathan Portis, *The Comeback Kid: The Life and Career of Bill Clinton* (New York: Birch Lane Press, 1992), p. 7.

5. Ibid, p. 10.

6. Ibid.

7. Ibid, p. 30.

8. Ibid.

9. Judith Warner, *Hillary Clinton: The Inside Story* (New York: Signet, 1993), p. 66.

10. Ibid, p. 57.

11. Allen and Portis, p. 36.

12. Warner, p. 58.

13. Ibid, p. 64.

14. Ibid, p. 62.

15. Ibid, p. 67.

16. Ibid, p. 71.

Chapter 6

1. Judith Warner, *Hillary Clinton: The Inside Story* (New York: Signet, 1993), p. 76.

2. Martha Sherrill, "The Rising Lawyer's Detour to Arkansas," *Washington Post,* Jan. 12, 1993, p. B1.

3. Charles F. Allen and Jonathan Portis, *The Comeback Kid: The Life and Career of Bill Clinton* (New York: Birch Lane Press, 1992), p. 36.

4. Ibid, p. 211.

5. Eleanor Clift, "'I Think We're Ready': Hillary Clinton speaks out about her family, her career and her marriage," *Newsweek,* Feb. 3, 1992, p. 21.

6. Allen and Portis, p. 211.

7. Sherrill, p. B1.

8. Clift, p. 21.

9. Warner, p. 83.

10. Ginny Carroll, Eleanor Clift, Howard Fineman and

Tom Morganthau, "Will Hillary Help or Hurt?" *Newsweek,* March 30, 1992, p. 31.

11. Warner, p. 84.

12. Sherrill, p. B2.

13. Warner, p. 87.

14. Allen and Portis, p. 211.

15. David Lauter, "Clinton Takes Sentimental Detour to Political Roots," *Los Angeles Times,* Oct. 22, 1992, p. A1.

16. Warner, p. 90.

Chapter 7

1. Judith Warner, *Hillary Clinton: The Inside Story* (New York: Signet, 1993), p. 91.

2. Ibid.

3. Ibid, p. 81.

4. Diane Blair, "Of Darkness and Light," in Ernest Dumas (ed.), *The Clintons of Arkansas* (Fayetteville: The University of Arkansas Press, 1993), p. 64.

5. Ibid, p. 65.

6. Warner, p. 93.

7. Ibid, p. 94.

8. Ibid, p. 96.

9. Ibid, p. 96.

10. Ibid, p. 95.

11. Kenneth T. Walsh, "He's not Barrister Bill," *U.S. News and World Report,* July 26, 1993, p. 32.

12. Charles F. Allen and Jonathan Portis, *The Comeback Kid: The Life and Career of Bill Clinton* (New York: Birch Lane Press, 1992), p. 51.

13. Stephen A. Smith, "Compromise, Consensus and Consistency," in Ernest Dumas (ed.), *The Clintons of Arkansas* (Fayetteville: The University of Arkansas Press, 1993), p. 12.

14. Eleanor Clift, "'I Think We're Ready': Hillary Clinton speaks out about her family, her career and her marriage," *Newsweek,* Feb. 3, 1992, p. 22.

15. Ibid.

16. Allen and Portis, p. 69.

Chapter 8

1. Diane Blair, "Of Darkness and Light," in Ernest Dumas (ed.), *The Clintons of Arkansas* (Fayetteville: The University of Arkansas Press, 1993), p. 67.

2. Judith Warner, *Hillary Clinton: The Inside Story* (New York: Signet, 1993), pp. 107–109.

3. Charles F. Allen and Jonathan Portis, *The Comeback Kid: The Life and Career of Bill Clinton* (New York: Birch Lane Press, 1992), p. 71.

4. Eleanor Clift, "'I Think We're Ready'" *Newsweek,* Feb. 3, 1992, p. 22.

5. Warner, p. 116.

6. Ibid, p. 115

7. Ibid, p. 116.

8. Allen and Portis, p. 78.

9. Ibid, p. 84.

10. Warner, p. 126.

11. Ibid, p. 128.

12. Allen and Portis, p. 189.

13. "60 Minutes" transcript, CBS, Inc., Jan. 26, 1992.

14. Ibid.

Chapter 9

1. Michael Barone, "Entering the Combat Zone," *U.S. News and World Report,* March 30, 1992, p. 39.

2. Margaret Carlson, "A Hundred Days of Hillary," *Vanity Fair,* June 1993, p. 169.

3. Judith Warner, *Hillary Clinton: The Inside Story* (New York: Signet, 1993), p. 191.

4. Patricia O'Brien, "The First Lady with a Career?" *Working Woman*, August 1992, p. 44.

5. Robin Toner, "Backlash for Hillary Clinton Puts Negative Image to Rout," *New York Times*, Aug. 24, 1992, p. A1.

6. Douglas Laycock, "What Hillary Clinton Really Said," *Wall Street Journal*, Dec. 16, 1992, p. A17.

7. Toner, p. A1.

Chapter 10

1. Jack Nelson, "Time for Sacrifice, Clinton Says: He Takes Oath, Calls for 'American Renewal'," *Los Angeles Times*, Jan. 21, 1993, p. A1.

2. R.W. Apple, Jr., "A Day of Dreams, a Time of Commitment: Clinton Starts With Nation's Good Wishes; His Task is to Retain Its Allegiance," *New York Times*, Jan. 21, 1993, p. A1.

3. Carl Sferrazza Anthony, *First Ladies: The Saga of the Presidents' Wives and Their Power, 1789–1961"* (New York: Quill/William Morrow, 1990), p. 551.

4. Richard Louv, "First, Family: Clinton has 3 ways to go on children, and advocates are in there pitching," *San Diego Union-Tribune*, Jan. 23, 1993, p. E1.

5. David E. Rosenbaum, "Hails and Farewells: An Emotional Gulf," *New York Times*, Jan. 21, 1993, p. A1.

6. Dotson Rader, "We Need a New System Now," *Parade*, April 11, 1993, p. 5.

Chapter 11

1. Matthew Cooper et al., "Co-President Clinton?" *U.S. News and World Report*, February 8, 1993, p. 30.

2. Patt Morrison, "Time for a Feminist as First Lady?"" *Los Angeles Times*, July 14, 1992, p. A1.

3. Ibid.

4. Walter Shapiro, "Whose Hillary is She, Anyway?" *Esquire,* August 1993, p. 86.

5. David Lauter, "Mrs. Wonk Goes to Washington," *Los Angeles Times Magazine,* May 23, 1993, p. 12.

6. "Backstage With Esquire," *Esquire,* August 1993, p. 17.

7. Shapiro, p. 86.

8. Margaret Carlson, "At the Center of Power," *Time,* May 10, 1993, p. 36.

9. Carlson, p. 170.

10. Michael Kelly "Hillary Rodham Clinton and the Politics of Virtue," *New York Times Magazine,* May 23, 1993, p. 22.

11. Ibid.

12. Ibid.

13. Michael Lerner, "Cynicism vs. the Politics of Meaning," *Los Angeles Times,* June 20, 1993, p. M5.

14. Kelly, p. 22.

15. Ibid.

16. Carlson, p 171.

17. Dotson Rader, "Hillary Rodham Clinton," *Parade,* April 11, 1993, p. 11.

18. Jill Brooke and Barbara Graustark, "At Home With Hillary Clinton," *Metropolitan Home,* November 1992, p. 24.

19. Carlson, p. 35.

Further Reading

If you would like to learn more about Hillary Rodham Clinton, look for these publications in your local library.

Books

Allen, Charles F, and Jonathan Portis. *The Comeback Kid: The Life and Career of Bill Clinton.* New York: Birch Lane Press, 1992.

Dumas, Ernest (ed.). *The Clintons of Arkansas.* Fayetteville: University of Arkansas Press, 1993.

Warner, Judith. *Hillary Clinton: The Inside Story.* New York: Signet, 1993.

Magazines and Newspapers

Carlson, Margaret. "At the Center of Power." *Time,* May 10, 1993, p 36.

Carlson, Margaret. "A Hundred Days of Hillary." *Vanity Fair,* June 1993, p. 170.

Kelly, Michael. "Hillary Rodham Clinton and the Politics of Virtue." *The New York Times Magazine,* May 23, 1993, p. 22.

Lauter, David. "Hillary in the Hot Seat." *Los Angeles Times Magazine,* May 23, 1993, p. 16.

Rader, Dotson. "We Are All Responsible." *Parade,* April 11, 1993, p. 4.

Sherrill, Martha. "The Education of Hillary Clinton: Her Journey From Goldwater Girl to First Lady." *Washington Post,* Jan. 11, 1993, p. B1.

Index